The Renewed Mind

THE RENEWED MIND

FRANS M. J. BRANDT

Copyright © 1982, 1984, 1999 by Dr. Frans M. J. Brandt.
All rights reserved

Printed in the United States of America

Published by WinePress Publishing
PO Box 428, Enumclaw, WA 98022.

No part of this publication may be reproduced, stored in a retrieval system, or transmitted in any way by any means—electronic, mechanical, photocopy, recording, or otherwise—without the prior permission of the copyright holder, except as provided by USA copyright law.

Please note: The contents of this book are not intended as a substitute for professional care and attention by a health professional. For example, it is always necessary to see a qualified physician before embarking on a new diet, exercise, or other physical health program. Any application of the discussions and/or recommendations in this book are at the reader's own discretion and sole responsibility.

Unless otherwise noted all scriptures are taken from the Holy Bible, New International Version, Copyright © 1973, 1978, 1984 by the International Bible Society. Used by permission of Zondervan Publishing House. The "NIV" and "New International Version" trademarks are registered in the United States Patent and Trademark Office by International Bible Society.

Cover illustration by Annette J. Blair, BFA, MA.

ISBN 1-57921-209-3
Library of Congress Catalog Card Number: 99-60156

For my son Peter Gerard

I am the light of the world. Whoever follows me will never walk in darkness, but will have the light of life.
—John 8:12

Acknowledgments

It is with great pleasure that I acknowledge my indebtedness to those who have helped me in the preparation of this book. For assistance with this newly revised edition, I am especially grateful to Kevin Lee, Andrea MacVay, Bill Stone, and John Vriend. May the Lord bless your dedication and diligence.

Contents

Foreword xiii
Preface xv

Part One
The Constructive Use of Our Mind

1. A Restless Longing 19
2. Helping Ourselves With God's Help 27

Part Two
The Power of Our Mind

3. Faith and Reason 35
4. Mind and Holy Spirit 43
5. Troubled but Not Distressed 51

Part Three
Understanding Our Mind

6. Understanding Our Emotions 57
7. Making Sound Decisions 67
8. Learning New Life-Enhancing Behavior 75

Part Four
A Sound Mind in a Sound Body

9. Emotional Problems May Have a Physical Basis 87
10. Some Definite Don'ts for Good Physical Health 103
11. Some Important Do's for Good Physical Health 115

Part Five
The Renewed Mind

12. Some Aspects of Unhealthy Personality Styles 129
13. Building a Healthy Personality Style 151
14. The Secret of Happiness 163
15. How to Have a Renewed Mind 181

References 197
Subject Index 199

Foreword

Dr. Frans Brandt has long been concerned about the all-important interaction of spirit, mind, and body. For almost two decades I have enjoyed working with him on various projects and have always found my own life enlightened and blessed because of his insights into human behavior, selfless dedication, and commitment to truth, reason, and faith.

"The renewing of the mind," the apostle Paul reminds us, "is essential for a transformed life." In my fifty years of ministry I have increasingly seen that the change of heart we encourage in our preaching truly demands an updated mind. We need a renewed mind—a Christian mind—if we are going to successfully deal with the powerful forces that seek to pollute our lives, cause our personalities to be unhealthy, contaminate our relationships, destroy our families, and pit individuals and nations against each other.

The first two editions of this book have found their way to many individuals across this nation and such far away places as the Middle East, Africa, India, and China. May God bless this newly revised edition likewise, have it reach deep into the hearts and minds of the readers, and inspire them to eagerly seek a transformed life.

William L. Stone, MDiv.

Preface

In this inspiring and remarkably clear synthesis of common sense and uncommon wisdom, Dr. Brandt takes us on a journey of personal wholeness. From the deep longing for joy residing in every heart, to the natural and scriptural laws through which God's loving grace has made such joy possible in our daily lives, we are invited on an exciting sojourn of personal spiritual transformation.

The intimate interrelationship of body, mind, and spirit has rarely been so thoroughly and practically revealed, as in *The Renewed Mind*. Reflecting the wisdom he has gleaned from a quarter century of clinical psychological counseling, Dr. Brandt's refreshingly readable and direct style is tempered with the compassion, reverence, and hopefulness with which he genuinely regards the whole of humanity.

Both the seasoned professional as well as the casual reader of *The Renewed Mind* cannot help but be swept away by Dr. Brandt's well-reasoned expositions of the spiritual anatomy of the transformed heart and mind. While this well-written text will serve the needs of the modern reader, for a thoroughly researched and comprehensive resource, the true source of illumination behind this work is to be found in Him who is truly "the light of the world."

Kevin H. Lee, DO

Part One:

The Constructive Use of Our Mind

1

A Restless Longing

For God is not a God of disorder but of peace.
—1 Cor. 14:33

We are standing on the threshold of the twenty-first century—a century already shining with bright hope and many promises for our restless world; where, in spite of incredible pain and problems, we can so clearly see an unfolding of God's wonderful and victorious plan of redemption. Looking back on the twentieth century, we remember the vicious onslaught humanity endured at the hateful hands of the powers of darkness. The evil perpetrated by these powers is deeply engraved on our hearts and rallies us even more strongly around the lifesaving light of the gospel. How wonderful to know that every evil thing ever undertaken by misguided individuals has failed. Darkness has no choice: It must succumb to light.

Today, the same as at the end of the last century, many individuals sincerely believe that civilization is about to collapse. After all, the most rudimentary review of world history unmistakably reveals that even the most powerful kingdoms and empires eventually fall into decline, and then into ruin. It is a major error, however, to confuse the demise of nations with the demise of civilization, and especially *Christian* civilization. Greece and Rome are no longer all-powerful. As nation states, they have long since lost influence and power, but their greatness in architecture, art, and literature is as much alive today as it ever was, and much of it was produced after their so-called decline.

Christianity, contrary to the opinions of some individuals, is flourishing greatly around the globe. No evil force, opposing power, or wayward ruler can hold back the penetrating rays of God's light and love. A nation that embraces such timeless and treasured godly values as goodness, justice, righteousness, and selflessness, discovers that these values cannot be eradicated.

The reverse also holds true. A nation that willingly embraces corruption, dishonesty, gambling, gluttony, greed, idolatry, immorality, substance abuse, and so forth, will discover that these evils will directly contribute to its decay and destruction from within. Nevertheless, the decline and even bankruptcy of a nation does not, can not, herald the demise of Christian civilization. God will not be limited by the follies of either individuals or whole nations. We can be assured of one thing: All is well on every front. God is alive, and His glorious light will shine upon all that lives and breathes.

Everything that has been achieved, and is being achieved, for the kingdom of God, will not only endure—it will prosper. While secular institutions and undertakings may disintegrate all around us, we will witness a continued, powerful move of God's Holy Spirit in all Christian endeavors. More and more Christians will catch the vision of God's endless grace and selfless love. This vision will lead to a growing unity among Christians, a refusal to be limited by denominational barriers, and a fervent desire to lift high the cross of Christ—to lift the light of the gospel high above chaos, confusion, disorder, fear, and lies being spread by the powers of darkness. "Looking at false teaching," writes Peter Jones, "makes the gospel even more convincing, and examining the lie causes the truth to sparkle in all its radiance, and with greater intensity" (Jones, 1997).

We do not listen to doubting, doomsayer, negative, or pessimistic voices seeking to intrude into our minds and wanting us to believe there is no future, no hope. God tells us differently: "For I know the plans I have for you, declares the Lord, plans to prosper you and not to harm you, plans to give you hope and a future" (Jer. 29:11). And what a wonderful future it is: saved by grace, justified by faith, sanctified by mercy, surrounded by love, endowed with power from on high, encouraged by the community of saints, and kept safely in the palm of God's hand. There is nothing whatsoever to fear in the future. The future for the Christian believer is brighter than ever. The new century will bring unparalleled growth to God's kingdom. We not only have more and more Christians, we have more and more committed Spirit-led and Spirit-filled Christians who are aglow with the gospel, and who are reaching not millions, but *billions* of individuals with "glad tidings of joy." Christian civilization has continued to blossom throughout some of the darkest centuries of our history, but in the twenty-first century, we will, more than ever before, experience the fullness of the gospel, the fruit of the Spirit, and the blessings of a transformed, victorious, and abundant life.

In the years ahead, there will be an increasing merger of evil with evil and good with good. But this we know from the Word of God, and have confirmed by history: Evil cannot last, and cannot win. Every year, every decade, every century hastens the final demise of evil, hastens the victory of good, hastens the coming of our Lord and Savior, and hastens the blessedness of eternal peace. We have an eager and restless longing for that day, but we are not to stand idly by and await its arrival. God wants us to be participators in His kingdom. We are to grapple earnestly with such issues as justice and mercy, wellness and wholeness, righteousness and sanctification. In the midst of our search for spiritual growth, or any other undertaking, we are to trust the Word of God, the guidance of the Holy Spirit, and the Lordship of Jesus Christ.

A Futile Search

During the past decades, we have witnessed scores of programs that sought to stem the tide of a seemingly endless increase in emotional problems. Dysfunctional anger, anxiety, and depression, in particular, have become a national problem. Tens of millions of individuals have been seeking, or are seeking, professional help to overcome personal or interpersonal unhappiness. In spite of many governmental, educational, and private programs, and the spending of billions of dollars on "medications," the emotional health of this nation continues to decline. In the meantime, millions of unhappy, and often desperate, individuals are frantically searching for a *modicum* of happiness in their lives.

Lacking insight into the nature of their predicament, unable to deal with the many stressors around them, and often devoid of a moral or spiritual anchor, millions of individuals are on a futile search. Futile, because they believe that the solution to their problem lies primarily in finding the right kind of medicine, partner, employment, or some other external factor. Futile, because a lasting solution to unhappiness can only be found in a fundamental and permanent change in our mental, emotional, and spiritual orientation.

We must rid ourselves of the misconception that we are merely helpless bystanders on the road to happiness, wellness, and success. We must rid ourselves of the notion that heredity and environment control our destiny—that we are mere pawns being moved across the chessboard of life by powerful external forces. While other individuals and many of life's events may provide various circumstances over which we can make ourselves happy or unhappy, the fact remains that most of us, at least in our society, have the final say over our emotional wellness.

The search for happiness, wellness, or wholeness is futile as long as we see ourselves as powerless bystanders, continue to believe that there are some kind of dividers, or "zippers," between our spiritual, emotional, and physical life, and fail to understand the power of our mind as a healer or a slayer. Unrealistic, irrational, and negative thinking hastens our demise, but realistic, rational, and optimistic thinking—constructive thinking—provides us with untold opportunities to choose wisely and become the sanctified kind of person God is looking for.

A More Fruitful Search

The Scriptures remind us that the manner in which we think is directly responsible for the happiness of our mind, and the health of our body, or the absence thereof (Prov. 14:30; 15:13; 16:24; 17:22). This is what I have said elsewhere:

> Every part of our body is subject to our mind, and every part of our mind is in some way influenced by, and dependent on, our body. In turn, both body and mind are subject to the power of God, who can heal instantaneously or gradually, with or without using health specialists. We cannot do anything to any part of our body, mind, or spirit that will not affect all three in some way. Because mental/emotional, and even spiritual wellness, intimately depends on a well-functioning body, there is every reason to pay special attention to proper nutrition and all other aspects of a healthy, well-balanced lifestyle. (Brandt, 1988)

In his letter to the Thessalonians, the apostle Paul ends with a heartfelt prayer that they be *completely* sanctified; not just spiritually, but also physically and emotionally (1 Thess. 5:23). God has always been concerned with our total being. We are to be *wholly holy* and dare not neglect any aspect of our tripartite make-up, be it spirit, mind, or body. The body, we are told, is the "temple of the Holy Spirit." It is also in charge of properly using food substances for the manufacture and distribution of chemicals and electricity that are necessary for healthy brain functioning. It is of the greatest importance that we fully understand that *a sound spiritual life is not possible without a sound mind*. Now the latter obviously needs a healthy brain, which in turn needs a well-nourished body. Needless to say, we must take an active part in our sanctification. For over twenty years, I have shared these insights with thousands of individuals and have never failed to see positive results in those who faithfully and wholeheartedly paid attention to the total person: spirit, mind, and body.

Every well-informed believer knows that at the root of spiritual malaise we can find sin of one kind or another, or we find a God-void, God-neglect, or God-confusion. None of this can be corrected with a handful of vitamins or ten minutes on an exercise bike! *God-void* calls for repentance of our sins and calling on the name of our Lord and Savior Jesus Christ (John 3:16; 3:36; 5:24; Rom. 10:13–17); *God-neglect* requires that we return to God and learn from the story of the prodigal son how much God rejoices when backsliders and rebels come home (Luke 15:3–32). *God-confusion,* on the other hand, requires that we allow the Holy Spirit to remind us that we are the children of God, saved and sanctified by Jesus Christ (1 Cor. 6:11). We must steadfastly reject any form of bondage, be it fear, doubt, or confusion (Rom. 8:15,16).

No one, however, can overcome his or her spiritual malaise when "strung out" on alcohol, illegal drugs, or anything else that makes our brain, and hence our mind, dysfunctional. We must be totally sanctified: spirit, mind, and body. That is the message of this book—a message that has helped many to happiness, wellness, and success, but more importantly, to a transformed life—a life that is pleasing to God and helpful to others.

It is important to remember that we are not in search of just any kind of happiness or good feeling. Without the Lordship of Jesus Christ, our happiness is like standing on shifting sand—an illusion that will disappear at a moment's notice. Without Jesus, our happiness rests only on physical and transient manifestations. Worldly happiness, at best is only a myth; and at worst, it will totally destroy us. The illusionary happiness of "the world" is quite different from the happiness we find in our Lord and Savior—a spiritual happiness that is complete, lasting, safe, and secure.

Our search for a joyful, meaningful, and purposeful existence can only be fruitful if we keep our eyes steadily on God the Father, Son, and Holy Spirit. We will increasingly be endowed with the healing power of His endless grace and selfless love. God wants us to be active participants on our road to spiritual and emotional maturity, and He emphasizes that we must "search, seek, ask, believe, and do." The choices God places before us are not burdens, but challenges; not hindrances, but opportunities. He has done everything that is needed for our happiness, and now we must choose.

2

Helping Ourselves with God's Help

> If any of you lacks wisdom, he should ask God, who gives generously to all without finding fault, and it will be given to him.
> —James 1:5

In the beginning of my counseling career, I was busily teaching others how they could help themselves to healthier and happier lives. One day, however, while attending a Christian seminar, the Holy Spirit convicted me that I was to teach others how to help themselves with the help of God. Happily, I understood why God wanted me to make this change.

All counseling, of whatever kind, is ultimately self-counseling. In a counseling setting, we absorb what others directly or indirectly, verbally or nonverbally, communicate to us. None of this, however, has the slightest effect on our lives, unless we, in one way or another, give ourselves verbal instructions to follow through on what we have heard and seen. It is not what others tell us that changes our lives, it is what *we tell ourselves* that counts. We always counsel ourselves—correctly or incorrectly. To counsel ourselves correctly, we must listen to the most reliable Counselor there is: the ". . . Wonderful Counselor, Mighty God, Everlasting Father, Prince of Peace . . ." (Isa. 9:6).

If I suggest to someone who has diabetes or hypoglycemia to stay away from candy, and that person *says to himself or herself,* "Dr. Brandt doesn't know what he is talking about; candy couldn't possibly hurt me," or "He may be right. I am going to stay away from candy," then through their thinking they are counseling *themselves*. Human beings counsel themselves continually. But, sadly, most of us seem to do this in a rather self-defeating way. If this was not so, we would not have jails and hospitals filled to overflowing with so many individuals who counseled themselves in a wrong manner. If most individuals were not counseling themselves wrongly (unrealistically, irrationally, and/or negatively), we could, at some future date, close most of our hospitals, and most of our physicians would be looking for other work. The simple truth is that 75 to 85 percent of all illnesses are the result of our faulty lifestyles, which in turn are mainly the result of incorrect "self-counseling." Fifty percent (one in two) of all Americans die before their time. God did *not* "call them home." He allowed this to happen.

In this country, more than three hundred thousand men and women annually kill themselves with tobacco smoking. Perhaps they first listened to "counseling" by manufacturers and advertising agencies telling them that it really is a "wonderful thing to smoke," and then they counseled themselves that, indeed, smoking is all right. If smokers listened to the "Wonderful Counselor," then they could learn to *say to themselves,* "My body is the temple of the Holy Spirit, and I am not going to willfully destroy it." Yes, it is a fact, we are the only ones who can help ourselves to happiness or unhappiness. It all depends on *how* we counsel ourselves. I am glad that God so clearly showed me that we must help ourselves with His help.

Christian Self-Counseling

The same week that I came home from that Christian seminar where God told me to "get with the program," I started a Christian self-counseling group at my church, began writing the first edition of this book, and not long thereafter, opened a Christian self-counseling center where we taught our clients how they could help themselves with God's help. Based on my experience, there is no better way to do counseling than teaching others how they can wisely counsel themselves; "teaching them to fish, rather than giving them an occasional fish."

Christian self-counseling is a practical method of emotional self-help, based on the Scriptures, and generally-accepted facts about some of the functions of the human mind, brain, and body. God, as we quickly discover in His Word, holds all *capable* persons responsible for their thoughts, feelings, and actions. He also shows us how we can make wise choices and lead happy, healthy, and productive lives. There is no question at all that God has placed us squarely in the driver's seat of life. He wants us to be drivers, not passengers; participators, not spectators.

In this temporal life, a life that is often unfair, we are forced to choose one thing over another. Failure to choose, however, is a choice, and usually not a very good one. The most constructive course of action is to choose wisely. Christian self-counseling gently reminds us that it is not only in our own best interest to live by truth, reason, and faith, but that this is pleasing to God and helpful to others. Since most of us are in the habit of counseling ourselves unwisely, it is necessary to make some fundamental changes in our thinking. For example, many of us erroneously believe that most unhappiness is caused by things we cannot control; by environmental events, or by other persons who "make" us angry, anxious, or depressed. As long as we cling to such misperceptions and misbeliefs, there is little hope for constructive self-counseling.

The Fruit of Our Lips

There is no doubt about this: *we are what we think,* and what we think, is, all too often, sheer nonsense. It is irrational thinking that gives us so many hardships. Not realizing that our "self-talk" (the way in which we first perceive and then interpret facts or events) creates our emotions, we mistakenly blame others for our angry, anxious, depressed, or other unwanted emotive feelings. Our greatest power is our power to choose—a power that can be used for good or bad. God insists that we use this power. He has given us the power to speak life or death, blessings or curses, into our existence: "The tongue has the power of life and death, and those who love it will eat its fruit" (Prov. 18:21).

What fruit are we eating? How are we counseling ourselves? Are we using life-giving self-talk and enjoying the fruit of happiness and joy? Are we using death-giving self-talk and reaping the fruit of anger and bitterness? We can instantly feel better if we shift our focus from negative to positive facts or events, from death to life, from sadness to joy, by the power of *our* tongue. Just try it. Start praising and thanking God for His blessings and for His endless, selfless, and steadfast love. Follow the advice from the Psalmist: "Give thanks to the LORD, for He is good. *His love endures forever*" (Ps. 136:1). Just thank our Heavenly Father, the Father of Light, the Spirit of love, the Creator of the universe, whose love conquered death and the grave, and who will never leave us nor forsake us. "For I am convinced," writes the apostle Paul, "that neither death nor life, neither angels nor demons, neither the present nor the future, nor any powers, neither height nor depth, nor anything else in all creation, will be able to separate us from the love of God that is in Christ Jesus our Lord" (Rom. 8:38,39).

If we are to succeed in any undertaking, we must remember that both success and failure spring from the same mind, the same lips: "From the fruit of his lips a man enjoys good things, but the unfaithful have a craving for violence" (Prov. 13:2). We truly are exactly what we think. If we think good thoughts, we will have good feelings and do good things. If we have angry, bitter, catastrophic, complaining, and demanding thoughts, we will have unhappy feelings and actions: "A fool's lips bring him strife, and his mouth invites a beating. A fool's mouth is his undoing, and his lips are a snare to his soul" (Prov. 18:6,7). Negative emotions, such as bitterness and malice, come from, and/or support, the powers of darkness who only seek to ". . . kill and destroy." We must be especially careful with negative self-talk, for it will bring us emotional, interpersonal, marital, physical, spiritual, vocational, and many other problems. "A crushed spirit," we are reminded, "dries up the bones" (Prov. 17:22).

Most individuals are quite capable of helping themselves (at least most of the time), with God's help, to happier, healthier, and more productive Christian lives. But we do need desire, faith, flexibility, open-mindedness, and willingness to succeed; nothing comes from nothing. God is at the helm, but we are to hoist the sails of our own ships. If we want to safely cross the turbulent seas of our lives, we must listen to God, apply His life-giving Word, praise Him from morning 'till night, pray without ceasing, and love selflessly. We must seek a transformed, victorious, and abundant life—a life that is fulfilling, joyful, and meaningful; a life marked by the "peace of God."

As I said earlier, all counseling ultimately is self-counseling, but we must make sure that it is *Christian* self-counseling. We must learn to make choices based on truth, reason, and faith. By giving us choice and volition, God has placed a tremendous challenge and a wonderful opportunity on our shoulders—an opportunity for responsible self-change. In the meantime, we know what He wants; He wants for us to make wise choices, be set free from perdition, walk in His light, and be endowed with power from above. God has provided everything; the tools are at hand. We have also been blessed with the knowledge that we are not mere end products of history—innocent victims of some cruel fate or the final outcome of conditioning. Later in this book, I will share how we can even alter unhealthy personality styles that may have developed in childhood or adolescence. We know that genetics and early-life experiences play an important part in forming our personalities, but God tells us, and history proves, that we can change. We can have a renewed mind and a transformed life!

Those who see human beings merely as helpless creatures in a long chain of evolutionary events, or the end products of physical and social development, make some big errors. They overestimate the power of the environment, underestimate the power of the mind, and, worst of all, don't know anything about the power of the Holy Spirit. We knowingly and joyfully reject the theory that we are wholly determined by the past. We know that we can have new minds, new personalities, newness of life; that we can be overcomers. We know that we are not the outcome of some accident, but a chosen people, the children of God, fellow-heirs with Christ, and endowed with the power of the Holy Spirit—God Himself, living within us.

In this book, we take a look at *reason* and *faith*, and the important interaction between *spirit, mind,* and *body*. We learn how to make sound decisions, how to have new behaviors, and how our mental health depends greatly on physical health. The more we look at the interdependence of our spiritual, emotional, and physical life, the more we come to understand God's urging to be *wholly sanctified*. That is our goal. Nothing less will do.

Part Two:

The Power of Our Mind

3

FAITH AND REASON

> By wisdom a house is built, and through understanding it is established.
> —Prov. 24:3

At first glance, it seems that faith and reason don't mix very well. After all, faith, from a Christian perspective, deals with a personal belief in God the Father, the self-existent, infinitely good and perfect Supreme Being, who created and preserves all things that have existence; God the Son, our Blessed Lord, who, by His death and suffering, has made atonement for our sins and saves all who believe in Him from eternal misery; and God the Holy Spirit, the third person of the Holy Trinity, whose peculiar office, as distinguished from the Father and Son, is sanctification and inspiration. Our Christian faith is a matter of yielding to the truth of Christianity and experiencing an inward assurance, or settled conviction.

Faith is sometimes confused with positive thinking, and while the latter is closely related to faith, it is not identical with it. Faith is a gift from God, but positive thinking is only a learned mental ability—an acquired skill. Sometimes positive thinking is misunderstood to mean that we can get whatever we firmly believe in. There is neither scriptural nor historical evidence for this. And what a good thing that is! If fallible and imperfect (not to mention sinful) human beings could get whatever they firmly believed in then we would soon live in utter chaos. Nevertheless, positive thinking is important for a healthy and productive life. It helps us to be constructive, definite, or optimistic, rather than destructive, doubtful, or skeptical—all characteristics of negative thinking and a source of much unhappiness.

Reason, our mental faculty to think logically and make sound decisions, is concerned with the validity and reliability of our thoughts. Here we can quickly see how important rational thinking is, even in matters of faith. Surely, blind faith is dangerous. If we were to believe everything others tell us (or everything we tell ourselves!), we would be in deep trouble. Our faith must not be contrary to reason, nor must our reason contradict our faith. Faith and reason are to go hand-in-hand: ". . . faith comes from hearing the message, and the message is heard through the word of Christ" (Rom. 10:17).

The Power of Faith

Faith is a gift from God. It is Christ who is the architect of both our faith and our salvation. It is Christ who chose us first (John 15:16), and it is by His faith that He lives within us. The Christian believer cries out with the apostle Paul, "I live by faith in the Son of God, who loved me and gave himself for me" (Gal. 2:20). Faith is a gift from God, but this does not mean we don't have to do anything to activate that gift in our lives. No one else can use that gift on our behalf; we must do this ourselves. Especially in matters of faith, we must use our minds correctly. For example, God cannot answer our prayers when we sabotage them by not saying what we mean, not meaning what we say, or not asking according to His will. We must be clear about the things we want.

We must learn to trust more fully in God's gift of faith; to stand firm, expect miracles, fight the good fight, ask boldly, and share ourselves readily with others. In Hebrews 11:1, we read that ". . . faith is being sure of what we hope for. . . ." This alerts us to the fact that faith is not something that comes without effort. Our rational mind makes it clear that we are to place our complete trust in God. It is by our reasoning faculties that faith becomes the cornerstone of our religious beliefs. These same faculties remind us that we are saved "by grace through faith" and justified and sanctified by faith. It is only through faith that we have continuous access to God's precious gifts and promises. Faith is not something that is forced upon us, rather, it is a gift from God—a gift we can use or neglect. The choice is ours.

This responsibility to choose—making up our own minds—is a serious task. Certainly there is every reason for us to choose as rationally as possible. We are forced to make many choices every day, and we know how difficult this process can be. The complexity of our world, the subjective nature of many issues, and our own fallibility, make it essential that we choose wisely. Happily, God gave us minds so that we can choose wisely. We do not have to be driven by some blind force. Although God gives us a choice, He insists that we be guided by truth, reason, faith, and love.

We need faith to have access to God's promises, and as long as we prepare ourselves mentally, we can receive these promises. The only thing that separates us from receiving God's promises is a lack of faith. This may reveal itself in self-defeating thinking and prevent us from reaching our goals. There is, however, enough guidance to go around by which we can help ourselves if we only look to God, the loving source of all good things. He tells us exactly what we need to do. "Ask and it will be given to you; seek and you will find; knock and the door will be opened to you" (Matt. 7:7). God calls, warns, teaches, and advises, but it is up to us to listen. He wants us to choose and take responsibility for our choices. God also uses pastors, teachers, counselors, and others, who may help, advise, counsel, guide, teach, and/or pray with us. Of course, we may spend years in so-called therapy and make no progress whatsoever. We can have the most rational advice and do the most irrational things. We can listen to the finest sermons, or be face to face with miracles, yet remain unmoved. The response is always ours.

The Power of Reason

Unless we take charge of our minds and counsel ourselves wisely, there will be no personal growth. Sadly, all too many individuals erroneously believe that they are not capable of thinking and choosing wisely. This is often the result of many years of wrong education or listening to the voice of the enemy, who exaggerates our weaknesses and minimizes our strengths. When we are repeatedly told that we are dumb and incapable of making decisions, we will become self-defeating in our thinking, feelings, and actions.

It is too bad that so many persons allow their environments (wives, husbands, children, friends, employers, or employees) to decide if they are going to be happy or not. For example, when our employer is in a bad mood, there is a good chance that we will also be in a bad mood; and when our employer is in a good mood, there is a good chance that we will also be in a good mood. This does not mean, however, that the environment is all-powerful. It means that if we do not take charge of our minds, we will be self-made victims of our environment. We will feel good when people like us (deservedly or not) and feel bad when they don't like us (deservedly or not), and, thus, we will be completely at their mercy. There is, however, no need for us to be emotionally at anyone's mercy, unless we choose to be.

We can choose to whom we will listen and what to do as a result. It is only through the use of reason that we can make decisions that are in our best interest. We counsel ourselves and can do so rationally or irrationally. All too often, we erroneously believe that our minds will simply take care of themselves. This is not true. Ideally our minds seek executive control from the Holy Spirit. Without guidance, our minds willingly absorb all manner of nonsensical and self-destructive information. The apostle Paul warns us, "Do not conform any longer to the pattern of this world, but be transformed by the renewing of your mind. Then you will be able to test and approve what God's will is—his good, pleasing, and perfect will" (Rom. 12:2). We can ask God to renew our minds, but that is not what God is telling us here. We have to update our own minds. God has already done His part; He is waiting for us to do our part. He wants us to choose, decide, reason, and be responsible. God will not refuse what He has promised, but it is up to us to lead lives that are pleasing to Him and beneficial to others. In order to succeed with Christian self-counseling, we must be involved and committed. What are those things in the world that we don't want to be conformed to? What is there in our lives that we need to change? Since *our* thinking is responsible for *our* feelings and actions, we directly control such negative events as smoking, overeating, and jealousy, and, of course, also the positive things that we feel and do. We *are* the end product of our thoughts.

Do we really wish to renew our minds and do God's "good, pleasing, and perfect will?" If so, we must pay attention to those things that prevent us from reaching that goal: negative and destructive thoughts and anything else that severs or hinders our relationship with God. Any thought, feeling, or action which harms our bodies or minds, so that we cannot be ". . . living sacrifices, holy and pleasing to God" (Rom. 12:1), is certainly against the will of God. It is the will of God that we love him and remember that He loved us first: . . . "But he was pierced for our transgressions, he was crushed for our iniquities; the punishment that brought us peace was upon him, and by his wounds we are healed" (Isa. 53:5). God wants us to understand that He has done His part.

How can we do our part? As Christians, we need to participate in the full development of our minds and our faith. God has provided the tools—reason, wisdom, and understanding, by which our minds can give strength and direction to our faith. We need to be as factual, rational, and hopeful, as possible—to live by truth, reason, faith, and love. Just look at Jesus. He was the most rational person who ever lived on earth. He did *nothing* that was self-defeating. Everything He did was true and objective. He did nothing harmful to His body, mind, or spirit. And when He gave His life for us, it was both a rational and loving act, for it fulfilled the will of God, and, among other things, led to His resurrection and glory (Luke 24:26). Jesus' life was goal-achieving and allowed Him to feel the way He wanted to feel. The difficulties He experienced with those who opposed Him were not significant to Him; He endured them without destructive anger, guilt, or worry, and remained steadfast. Only the Son of God can be completely rational, but, we are to follow His example and live by truth, reason, faith, and love.

The Power of Faith and Reason

When we do self-defeating things, it is not always the result of unholiness. Frequently, we are simply uninformed or misinformed. Perhaps we don't know any better because we were unable to learn, or did not have an opportunity to do so. Ignorance, however, is not really bliss. Not knowing may get us into serious trouble with ourselves or with others. For some of our ignorance, we may have an excuse, especially if we did not have an opportunity to learn. Much of our ignorance, however, is inexcusable. If only we would spend as little as ten minutes a day, we could make major improvements in our lives. We could eliminate many misunderstandings, biases, prejudices, and unhealthy personality traits from our lives.

So much of our behavior toward God is unreasonable as well. Does it make sense to ask God to forgive us our transgressions if we fail to accept His forgiveness? Should we ask God to help us feel better about ourselves if we continue to blame ourselves? How can we expect God to rescue us if we insist that we are worthless? How can God take away our depressions when, day and night, we talk endlessly about the terrible, horrible, and awful things that always happen to us? If we continue to dwell on bad things, it is impossible to have a renewed mind. Jesus reminds us that: ". . . out of the overflow of the heart the mouth speaks. The good man brings good things out of the good stored up in him, and the evil man brings evil things out of the bad stored up in him. But I tell you that men will have to give account on the day of judgment for every careless word they have spoken. For by your words you will be acquitted, and by your words you will be condemned" (Matt. 12:34–37).

The Scriptures remind us that "death and life are in the power of the tongue." We must closely guard our mouths. For the resolution of our problems we need faith, but our faith has to make sense.

We must remember that faith is "being sure of what we hope for and certain of what we do not see" (Heb. 11:1). What are some of the things we hope for in our lives? God wants us to lead joyful lives, but are we actively choosing this? To have more control over our feelings and actions, we need both faith and reason. God specifically warns us to reject "blind faith." A rational faith is not based on feelings, but on fact. It is important to remember ". . . faith comes from hearing the message, and the message is heard through the word of Christ" (Rom. 10:17). The deeper our faith is anchored in a *rational mind,* the more fruitful it will be. Our reasoning minds will strengthen our faith in God and give us more enjoyable lives here on earth.

God wants us to live by faith and reason, grounded in truth, and expressed in love.

This is what I stated elsewhere:

> Right thinking—thinking rooted in God's perspectives on human life—is oriented to truth. It does not wish to wear blinders. It is open to the reality which heals body, mind, and spirit. The ultimate in right thinking is to think as God thinks. "Let this mind be in you, which was also in Christ Jesus" (Phil. 2:5). Christ did not stand upon his privileges, but as the Bible vividly puts it ". . . took the form of a servant . . ." (Phil. 2:7). This is the model for right thinking. (Brandt, 1988)

There can be no mistake about this—the faith of God implanted into our hearts is far more superior than our power to reason. Faith and reason are both important, but faith—the faith of God—is obviously the more important ingredient: "For it is by grace you have been saved, through faith—and this not from yourselves, it is the gift of God—not by works, so that no one can boast" (Eph. 2:8, 9).

There is no question at all that faith can overcome many of the limitations of reason. Through the constructive use of our minds, however, we discover that our faith acts when we get into action. It helps us focus on the important guidance that we can obtain from the Word of God.

4

Mind and Holy Spirit

≈◆≈

> . . . stay in the city until you have been clothed with power from on high.
>
> —Luke 24:49

In the previous chapters, we have talked about the importance of making wise choices and the interrelationship of faith and reason. We also reiterated that our thinking is primarily responsible for our feelings and actions. Right thinking—constructive thinking—we found, produces life-enhancing feelings and actions. Since right thinking is vital for our happiness and wellness, it is no wonder there are so many scriptures on this subject. The book of Proverbs, for example, overflows with reminders to think and speak right: to guard our lips, refrain from harsh words, not ensnare our souls with our lips, and have happy thoughts for cheerfulness.

"The tongue," we read in Proverbs 18:21, "has the power of life and death, and those who love it will eat its fruit." We must learn to master the life-giving power of pleasant words—words that are affectionate, cheerful, cooperative, encouraging, generous, genuine, honest, kind, merciful, optimistic, peaceful, respectful, reasonable, soothing, and, above all else, selfless. We cannot have happy or healthy lives unless we take responsibility for our thoughts. For fallible, imperfect, and sinful human beings, however, this is not an easy task. We may want to be more responsible and have more joyful lives but may find it difficult to do. We need some help; our minds need guidance!

Since our thinking controls our minds, we may want to ask, "Who and what controls our thinking?" "What standards, values, and objectives guide our thinking?" "How are we dealing with our genetic, environmental, social, physical, or other limitations?" "How do we deal with the fact that our minds do not automatically make right choices and decisions for us?" Everything we do in life, ultimately, is the result of what we feed into our minds. Regrettably, many individuals are unaware of that responsibility. They will blame others for their feelings and behaviors, failing to recognize the power of personal choice. Happily, we are not the end products of our environments. We are not mere robots or puppets. We are made by history only to the extent that we allow this to be so, particularly in the area of our spiritual and emotional health.

If our minds were the smart, self-regulating entities that so many persons believe them to be, our lives would be happy and healthy most of the time. Without proper guidance, however, our minds become doubtful, fearful, or confused. We need sound executive control over our minds. We need to be directed by "power from on high"—a power that enables us to have peace, joy, and righteousness in our lives. We need to carefully, consciously, and wisely use our minds with the guidance of the Holy Spirit. This guidance will be reflected in what is known as a "Spirit-filled life."

The Spirit-Filled Life

The Spirit-filled life is the Christ-centered life. It results from giving control of our mind to the Holy Spirit. Who is the Holy Spirit? The Holy Spirit is the third person of the Trinity. The concept of one God who has existed from all eternity in three distinct—not separate—persons, is difficult to grasp. In fact, we cannot grasp it fully, because we are finite beings. But we can affirm and experience the reality of the Holy Spirit's presence in our lives. The Holy Spirit *speaks to* (Acts 13:2), *intercedes for* (Rom. 8:26), *testifies to* (John 16:26), *leads* (Rom. 8:14), *guides* (John 16:13), and, in general, *directs* the life of the believer. The Holy Spirit is *God eternal* (Heb. 9:14), *all-powerful* (Luke 1:35), *present everywhere* (Ps. 139:7), and *all-knowing* (1 Cor. 2:10,11). We must increasingly seek the Spirit-filled life because it is the sensible, the wisest, yes, the only obedient thing to do. The apostle Paul insists on it. We have a choice, he says, between being filled with the addictive substances of this world and the highs they give us, or being filled with, and, therefore controlled and altered by, the Holy Spirit. The former, of course, is totally destructive of our personality and relations with others, while the latter enables us to sing and give thanks (Eph. 5:18–21). As Christians, we have no choice but to opt for the latter.

The Importance of a Healthy Mind

With the help of the Holy Spirit, it is not difficult to increase our faith to the point of believing and receiving. But we must use our minds and become committed, receptive, faithful, and loyal participators. It is only through correct choices that we live Christian lives. Without healthy, constructive minds, we cannot walk in the Spirit. It is a well-known fact that many of our destructive and self-defeating behaviors are the result of stupidity and ignorance. We need a healthy mind for a healthy walk in the Holy Spirit; we must live realistic and rational lives. Consider the life of Jesus: As God in human form, He was the most rational person who ever lived on earth. It is important to recognize that fact! The Lord was an active, thinking, participant. He prayed, taught, traveled, worked, studied, resisted temptations, performed miracles, and gave executive control of His mind to the Holy Spirit. God the Father, the Holy Spirit, and Jesus are one; yet, Jesus did not merely rely on his own judgment. He constantly and consistently looked to God the Father and the Holy Spirit for guidance.

It is only through the power of the Holy Spirit that we can choose to have a renewed mind. Of course, the opposite is also true. We can choose to give executive control of our minds to Satan by participating in the occult, relying on horoscopes or fortune tellers, or participating in seances. Or, we can forget our minds entirely and just flounder around, ignoring God's warnings and paying no attention to where we are going.

If Jesus, the Son of the living God, who Himself *is* God, consciously sought guidance from God the Father and God the Holy Spirit, then how much more are we in need of this! It is certainly at our peril if we ignore our need to be fed spiritually.

The Holy Spirit Cannot Dwell in a Carnal Mind

Our minds are astonishingly powerful. We can resolve and overcome some of the most devastating problems through the power of our mind and accomplish seemingly impossible tasks. Yet, all of these feats are nothing compared to the power that comes from the Holy Spirit. In this book, we will consider some simple steps that may enable us to overcome anxiety, depression, dysfunctional anger, and many other negative things. Such victory is wonderful and positive. Yet, a greater victory can be obtained by the power of the Holy Spirit, which comes to us through Jesus, as explained by John the Baptist: ". . . I baptize you with water. But one more powerful than I will come, the thongs of whose sandals I am not worthy to untie. He will baptize you with the Holy Spirit and with fire" (Luke 3:16).

God bestows the Holy Spirit on all believers at the time of salvation (Acts 10:44–48) and as a special anointing thereafter (Acts 19:1–7). Jesus makes it clear that *no believer will be denied the Holy Spirit*—He is there for the asking (Luke 11:13). Every Christian is to seek the guidance of the Holy Spirit. He will guide us and help us solve any and all problems, challenges, and difficulties! What we cannot achieve by the power of our mind is often achieved by the power of the Holy Spirit. We can do so, however, only if we truly seek a "spiritual mind." There is a great enmity between the carnal and spiritual mind (Rom. 8:7). It is a battle between good and evil; right and wrong; between constructiveness and destructiveness. The carnal mind can only bring pain, unhappiness, turmoil, and destruction. It embraces ". . . sexual immorality, impurity and debauchery; idolatry and witchcraft; hatred, discord, jealousy, fits of rage, selfish ambition, dissensions, factions and envy; drunkenness, orgies, and the like . . ." (Gal. 5:19–21). Many individuals are destroying their lives with their carnal behaviors. In our society, we find that rage, drunkenness, involvement with the occult, paganism, sexual immorality, and discord are common behaviors.

The Holy Spirit Seeks Willing Minds
God gives us a choice to either have a carnal mind *or* a spiritual mind, walk in light *or* darkness, be endowed with power *or* remain powerless. The most rational choice, obviously, is to seek a spiritual mind. Sadly, human beings are inherently irrational. All evidence throughout history—including our own lives—testifies to our irrational tendencies. Left alone as infants, we literally destroy ourselves. Left uneducated, we do not survive. It is not only our irrational nature, however, that is such a big problem, but our sinful nature—our selfishness and other sins. Human beings need guidance: They need a "flight plan."

No space shuttle goes up or comes down safely without a meticulous flight plan; likewise, none of us "do well" unless we obey God's flight plan to guide us safely—day by day, hour by hour, and moment by moment. Without knowledge, we cannot fly a space shuttle, and without knowledge, we cannot do a good job with our mental, emotional, or spiritual lives. In Proverbs 4:5, we are told to get wisdom and understanding. Such wisdom includes loving and obeying God and our neighbors. God is love, and we can know God and do His will and work, only through love. In Matthew 22:36–40 we read:

> Teacher, which is the greatest commandment in the Law? Jesus replied: "'Love the Lord your God with all your heart and with all your soul and with all your mind.' This is the first and greatest commandment. And the second is like it: 'Love your neighbor as yourself.' All the Law and the Prophets hang on these two commandments."

THE RENEWED MIND

God is selflessly committed to us. He wants us to be committed to Him also. God loves us even though we are *fallible* (liable to fail), *imperfect* (not completely good), and *sinful* (given to violate God's standards). God fully understands our fallibility and imperfections, but rejects our sinful behaviors, and so must we. But, when God forgives us, we must also forgive ourselves. How can we be happy or successful if we see ourselves as incompetent, incapable, inadequate, or worthless? How can an unwilling or self-condemning mind be "endowed with power from on high?" Let us be honest. It is impossible to listen to the Holy Spirit if we live in sin, and it is equally impossible to do so if we live with self-rejection, self-doubt, or self-hatred. The Holy Spirit can only work with a mind committed to right thinking and right living. Listen to what S. D. Gordon (1903) wrote nearly a hundred years ago:

> ". . . the Holy Spirit is power. . . . Power is a person. Not some thing, nor influence, nor sentiment, nor some working upon our hearts at a distance by God seated up yonder on the throne. That were wonderful indeed. But a person, called the Holy Spirit, living in me—shall I make it very definite by saying, living *in my body?*—that is power. If restrained by sin, or disobedience, or ignorance, or willfulness of any kind, then power restrained, given free sway and control—ah! Then power manifest, limitless, wonderful, all exercised in carrying out God's will in, and with, and through me. We can soar at heights without limit when our minds are directed by the Holy Spirit. The evidence of the Holy Spirit in one's life, however, may differ widely in different persons." (1 Cor. 12:4–6,11)

Gordon (1903) points out that Jesus' death and resurrection make it possible for us to be free from sin, but that it is the Holy Spirit dwelling within us who changes possible freedom into actual freedom. "Jesus," writes Gordon, "does in me now by His Spirit what He did for me centuries ago on the cross, in His person." Without the Holy Spirit, we are spiritually powerless. We may, for example, lack the ability to boldly, and convincingly, live and share the gospel: "For we know, brothers loved by God, that he has chosen you, because our gospel came to you not simply with words, but also with power, with the Holy Spirit and with deep conviction" (1Thess. 1:4,5).

Christian believers must eagerly seek the power of the Holy Spirit in their lives. Dozens of scriptures remind us of the importance of the Holy Spirit (e.g. John.14:16,23; 15:26; 16:13,14; Acts 1:4; 4:12; 4:31–37; 7:55,56; 10:44–46; Rom. 8:15; Gal. 4:6; 5:24,25; 2 Tim. 3:16; 2 Pet. 1:20,21). These scriptures also remind us that every infilling of the Holy Spirit always results in a deeper walk with God: a greater love for Him and others; a greater desire to serve Him; and many other manifestations of the gifts and fruits of the Holy Spirit. All of these, it must be noted, are always demonstrated in a selfless love for others and true devotion to Christ.

We must also be on guard, however, for false prophets in sheep's clothes (Matt. 7:15–23) and those evil doers who come disguised as "miracle workers," displaying ". . . all kinds of counterfeit miracles, signs, and wonders, and in every sort of evil that deceives those who are perishing . . ." (2 Thess. 2:9,10).

True servants of Christ are humble and selfless. They selflessly seek to save the lost and heal the sick. They minister not for "filthy lucre," or for self-aggrandizement, but for the glory of God and His Kingdom. We need to recognize that our body is the temple of the Holy Spirit, and that our mind is the heart—the command center—of that temple. We need a rational and willing mind to correctly and readily yield to the assurance, comfort, guidance, inspiration, and sanctification of the Holy Spirit.

5

Troubled but Not Distressed

We are hard pressed on every side, but not crushed
—2 Cor. 4:8

We live in a bipolar world—a world that is very beautiful, enjoyable, and inspiring, as well as complex, disheartening, and unfair. No human being on this planet can escape the reality of being affected, in one way or another, by the good and evil that surrounds them. Any attempt to escape this reality is doomed to failure; we cannot jump ship, and we cannot hide from ourselves.

Every human being, rich or poor, strong or weak, sooner or later finds himself or herself "troubled on every side." Happily, most human beings can be very creative, flexible, and pliable. Every day millions of individuals successfully deal with many challenging personal or environmental difficulties, hardships, or limitations. They do this in a variety of ways: by taking their eyes off themselves and helping others; replacing self-defeating beliefs with life-enhancing ones; focusing on the power of choice; and, steadfastly looking to God, the ultimate source of encouragement, inspiration, and strength.

The Power of Choice

It is true, of course, that we have no control over certain things in our lives, and it is also true that serious difficulties can come into our lives at any moment. But, glory to God, we have a tremendous choice as to *how we respond* to life's challenges: "We are hard pressed on every side, but not crushed; perplexed, but not in despair; persecuted, but not abandoned; struck down, but not destroyed" (2 Cor. 4:8,9).

How wonderful that *most* of us, *most* of the time, are quite capable of taking charge of our lives. In fact, we are commanded to do so (Deut. 30:19). *God holds all capable persons responsible for their actions* (Josh. 24:15). We are given an opportunity to choose for ourselves, but can only do so wisely with sound minds and guidance from the right sources. The ultimate right source for believers is, of course, the Holy Spirit.

We live in a world where God leaves it up to us to choose between two forces— good and evil. In order to be victorious over evil, we *must* make sound decisions and evaluate the various choices that are placed before us. While it is not possible to live our lives without conflict or difficulties, it is possible to eliminate a great deal of misery that comes from our failure to choose wisely. Even major emotional difficulties are not necessarily the end of things. We may look at the entire matter from God's perspective and say with the apostle Paul that "we are hard pressed, but not crushed." We may be down but also ready to get up!

Emotive feelings result from the way in which we evaluate and interpret facts or events, and these are open to evaluation and interpretation. In this way, many individuals have successfully dealt with some of the most severe physical, emotional, intellectual, social, and other handicaps. For example Joni Eareckson Tada (*Joni*, 1976), who, although paralyzed, reminds us in her moving and inspiring autobiography ". . . that in all things God works for the good of those who love him, who have been called according to his purpose" (Rom. 8:28). There are many persons who are either totally or partially healed, and others who are *not* healed, but who nevertheless can say with Paul ". . . I delight in weaknesses, in insults, in hardships, in persecutions, in difficulties. For when I am weak, then I am strong" (2 Cor. 12:10).

For the steadfast believer in Christ, there is meaning in life, and there is meaning in death; meaning in health, and meaning in affliction. It is wonderful that we can use our minds to act, rather than react; to be partakers, rather than spectators; to look above and beyond ourselves. Nothing of any kind can separate us from the love of God if only we are steadfast; if only we are courageous. Happily, there is no jail, there are no bonds, there is nothing by which we can be separated from God, as long as we trust in Christ. We can direct our thoughts and hence select our feelings.

We place meaning into our lives by the choices *we* make and by availing ourselves of opportunities—big or small, many or few. True happiness in life does not require any human power, wealth, or influence. Helen Keller, though blind and deaf, was a very happy person, and Joni Eareckson Tada, although paralyzed, is a happy person who is far more productive than many of us who have no physical limitations at all. And there are so many others, who, in spite of serious limitations, have led, or are leading, happy and constructive lives.

The Power of Doing

The good news of the gospel is only good news if we acknowledge and confess our sins, regret them, stop doing them, believe in Christ, and do the "will of God." There is no good news for us unless we do something to make this good news come true in our lives. Far too many people are talking about the "good news" and erroneously believe that Jesus is an "automatic ticket" to heaven. Nothing is further from the truth. We must be participators and consciously take a stand for salvation and sanctification.

God provides many opportunities to choose life, but He does not choose for us. Our needs are met only as long as we choose to do so. The most important word in the English language by which we can help ourselves to spiritual, mental, and physical happiness has only two letters: *do. We need to do something.* We are to help ourselves with God's help. We may need to replace some of our old thought patterns with new ones before we can acquire happier and healthier feelings and actions. In this book are some useful suggestions on how we can have more desired behavior, but we are the only ones who can do so. We can, for example, have more happiness, wellness, and success, if we stop restricting our lives within the self-limiting borders of self-pity and self-blame. Also, we can teach ourselves to be more truthful, accept more responsibility, and remind ourselves that we are just as capable of being constructive as destructive!

How wonderful that we can stop complaining, griping, blaming, or feeling sorry for ourselves. How marvelous that by changing our thoughts we can change our feelings. What a tremendous power is within our reach when we realize that "Pleasant words are a honeycomb, sweet to the soul and healing to the bones" (Prov. 16:24). What a blessing to give executive control of our mind to the Holy Spirit and enjoy a peace which goes beyond our understanding. How fantastic that we can rise above our difficulties and look beyond our afflictions, conflicts, difficulties, disappointments, frustrations, and other troubles. Thank God that we can wholeheartedly, and with full conviction, cry out that we have heard and do know that our Heavenly Father ". . . gives strength to the weary and increases the power of the weak" (Isa. 40:28–31). We may be troubled, but we are not distressed. As overcomers in Christ, we are always ready to get up one more time, every time!

Part Three:

Understanding Our Mind

6

Understanding Our Emotions

. . . and how good is a timely word!
—Prov. 15:23

It has been known throughout the centuries that thoughts, beliefs, attitudes, and mental images are the basis of human emotions. Our thoughts and beliefs, we have learned, can create helpful or destructive emotive feelings, and, as such, they can make or break us, build us up or tear us down. The process of selecting and creating the emotions we desire to have is not complicated, but, regrettably, many individuals fail to take advantage of this.

One reason why many individuals don't bother to create more desirable emotions is easy to understand. They sincerely believe that their emotions result from external, rather than internal, circumstances. They observed early in life that whenever someone was kind to them they felt happy or secure, and whenever someone was unkind to them they felt sad or insecure. Feelings, they concluded, are an external matter; the outcome of certain facts or events, and, in particular, of what other persons do, or don't do, to us. It's a very good thing that they are wrong in their assessment, but it's a very bad thing that they don't know this!

An Emotion Has Three Parts

Our emotions consist of *perceptions, thoughts,* and *feelings.* Our mental thoughts become our physical feelings. Although other factors also influence this process, our emotions are, ultimately, the outcome of our thinking. If we think negative thoughts, we have negative feelings. If we think happy thoughts, we have happy feelings. If we think depressive thoughts, we have depressive feelings. Whenever we alter our thinking, we alter our emotions. In a later chapter, we will consider the role that physical factors play in our emotional life.

The Emotion of Anger

Anger is a strong reactive feeling of displeasure over real or imaginary wrongs, injustices, or injuries—to ourselves or others—with or without concurrent impulses to retaliate. Anger is a controversial emotion in our society. Some individuals believe that it is always wrong to be angry. Others, including most Christians, make a clear distinction between assertive (righteous) anger and aggressive (nonrighteous) anger. Righteous anger, they believe, plays an especially important role in the protection and well-being of vulnerable individuals, as well as society as a whole.

The viewpoint that anger is always an inappropriate emotion seems incorrect and unbiblical. In the Old Testament, for example, there are at least three hundred instances where God Himself is very angry. He is angry at sin, human brutality, and destructiveness. In my opinion, the more correct viewpoint about righteous anger is summed up best by the apostle Paul. In his letter to the Ephesians in chapter four verse twenty-six, he cites Psalm 4: "In your anger do not sin. Do not let the sun go down while you are still angry . . ." There is, of course, a day and night difference between assertive anger and aggressive anger. The latter has no redeeming qualities of any kind. Aggressive anger seeks to blame, dissolve, harm, hurt, or incriminate. Frequently, this kind of anger is intertwined with a physical problem and/or a personality disorder. We will look at this in a later chapter.

Understanding Our Emotions

When it comes to aggressive anger (regardless of the various sources that may be at work), we find, once again, that the Scriptures have the right answers. We learn that our Heavenly Father wants us to change *cruelty* into *kindness; hardness* into *tenderness; hostility* into *friendliness; rudeness* into *politeness; ridicule* into *respect; persecution* into *support; contempt* into *courtesy; condemnation* into *pardon;* and *hatred* into *love*. Through actively combining knowledge, wisdom, and faith, we can ultimately be victorious, even over aggressive anger.

Most of our inappropriate anger is the result of anger-specific self-talk. As long as we continue to demand that certain facts or events *must, should, or ought to* be different than they realistically are or can be, then we will continue to make ourselves angry. To remedy this, we must carefully consider our thoughts, beliefs, and attitudes. We may find common thinking errors, such as *arbitrary inferences* (wrongly assuming that others have ulterior motives), *mind reading* ("supernaturally" knowing what others are thinking), and *selective abstraction* (focusing on what supports our biases and prejudices).

The Emotion of Anxiety

Anxiety is another very common emotion experienced by millions of normal individuals. At times, however, anxiety is quite disabling. As in the case of anger, there might be physical, psychological, as well as spiritual sources for our anxiety. Anxiety disorders, such as *panic, generalized anxiety, phobic, obsessive-compulsive,* and *post traumatic stress disorder*, require professional help. This help is widely available in this country. Anxiety disorders are eminently treatable.

In this chapter, we are focusing on normal anxiety, which can be described as a feeling of apprehensiveness, or uneasiness, about some unclear demand or a possible threat to our well-being. With anxiety, we are not really sure why we feel the way we do, whereas with fear we are sure. Fear is situation-specific. Normal anxiety, as experienced by healthy individuals, is not disabling, and at times may even spur us into necessary action. There are, however, also occasions when we feel far too anxious.

Excessive anxiousness interferes with our normal day-to-day activities and may be the result of excessive stress, an illness, or, more commonly, errors in our thoughts, beliefs, and attitudes. Common thinking errors that may lead to anxiety include *arbitrary inferences* (drawing conclusions in the absence of sufficient evidence), *catastrophizing* (overemphasizing a worst possible outcome), and *overgeneralization* (basing conclusions on scanty data).

Some fifty different physical conditions may play a role in anxiety-related problems, but, as a rule, anxiety (as stated earlier) is more likely the direct result of anxious thoughts and beliefs than of physical sources. Nevertheless, it is always important to obtain a thorough medical evaluation. It is folly to think that anxiety is *always* self-induced. It is not. Having said all of this, let us be mindful that anxious thoughts will lead to anxious feelings. And, in addition, let us not overlook the fact that anxiety can also result from spiritual problems.

What a difference we may notice in the calm demeanor of those who walk closely with God and the disquieting and perplexing uneasiness that is often found in those who walk without Him. All too many individuals are anxious about material possessions, personal power, status, or influence. Individuals with certain unhealthy personality styles, and those who live without meaning or purpose, will more readily experience the world as an uncertain, fearful, or dangerous place. Living in this world, without a secure relationship with God, may lead to experiencing the God-void we mentioned in a previous chapter. But Christians, too, may suffer from spiritual anxiety when they neglect God ("I am too busy") or are confused about God ("God does not care about me").

The antidote for anxiety *disorders* (versus normal anxiety) is usually found in medications and sound counseling. But the antidote for *spiritual anxiety* can only be found in God Himself. If we are anxious, afraid, or worried, then we must first seek the will of God. We can best do that by truly caring for the welfare and well-being of others. The Scriptures remind us that "God comforts us in all our troubles, so that we can comfort those in any trouble with the comfort we ourselves have received from God (2 Cor. 1:4). The Holy Spirit is our Comforter, Helper, and Healer. He is the true antidote for our anxieties. He reminds us to join thanksgiving to our prayers: "Do not be anxious about anything, but in everything, by prayer and petition, with thanksgiving, present your requests to God" (Phil. 4:6).

The Emotion of Depression

The third emotion to consider is *depression*. This rather common, unhappy, mental state often results from a fairly recent, real or perceived, significant *lack* or *loss*, in our life. Depression is characterized by prolonged and/or repeated periods of isolation, loneliness, sadness, self-blame, self-pity, and/or withdrawal. In addition, we may suffer with sleep difficulties and/or appetite and weight control problems. Readily identifiable "lacks" are usually accompanied by very specific self-defeating beliefs, such as: *lack of self-esteem* ("I am a worthless person"), *lack of control* ("I feel helpless"), *lack of faith* ("I don't think anything will ever change"), *lack of energy* ("I am always tired"), *lack of self-sufficiency* ("I need others to take care of me"), *lack of ability* ("I am stupid"), *or, lack of security* ("I am unprotected).

Depression is to be distinguished from *depressive illness,* which is a more severe form of depression and is usually the outcome of a genetic predisposition and/or a combination of a biochemical imbalance with self-defeating thinking. Depressive illness is characterized by morbid sadness, feelings of helplessness, hopelessness, or worthlessness, impaired thinking, suicidal thoughts, and major changes in appetite, sleep, or sexual desire patterns. Two common types of depressive illnesses are *bipolar disorder* (with both depressive and manic episodes) and *unipolar disorder* (recurrent depressive episodes).

Depression must also be distinguished from a *depressive personality style or disorder*. A depressive personality style is usually the outcome of multiple and/or prolonged negative experiences in childhood or early adolescence. Those who have a depressive personality rarely remember when this first began. It seems to them that they have always felt negative, pessimistic, or quickly defeated.

In this chapter, however, we must limit ourselves to a discussion of depression. Here is what I have said elsewhere:

> Depression is a multifaceted disorder of body, mind, and/or spirit. It is caused by excessive stress, which results in loss of physical balance, psychological integrity, and/or spiritual direction. It is not stress itself or stressful situations that get us into trouble, but the way in which we react to them. What causes depression in one person might not cause depression in another, and what heals one person might not heal another. That is why singular approaches and universal claims are ineffective, inappropriate, and often dangerous.
>
> We do not become depressed because of external lack, and/or loss, but very specific, individually determined, internal lack and/or loss. We become depressed as a result of ways in which each uniquely different body, mind, and/or spirit reacts to potential stressors. It is strictly our inability and/or unwillingness to successfully deal with potential stress that converts it into actual stress. Human beings are basically geared for survival, health, and healing. God has provided us with built-in physical and mental protective systems that enable us to live in an often hostile and unaccommodating world. The question to consider in dealing with the cause of depression is to what extent are we talking about vulnerability (ability versus inability) and choice (willingness versus unwillingness)? It will then become evident that indeed excessive stress is the real culprit behind our national epidemic of depression. Yet it is important to remember that we ultimately choose to control or not to control our stress levels. We have the final word.
>
> In the case of *physical stress*, it is primarily our physical condition that determines whether or not we are going to suffer loss of physical balance. The better our health, the greater the amount of stress we will be able to endure. In the case of *psychological stress*, it is primarily our perceptual-cognitive field that turns potential stressors into actual ones. The more rationally, realistically, and positively integrated we are, the less likely will po-

tential stressors become actual stressors. The greater the ability and willingness to reason, and the greater our desire for realism and optimism, the more able we are to deal with psychological stress, and thus prevent loss of psychological integration. In the case of *spiritual stress*, it is primarily our willingness to yield our imperfect will to the perfect will of God. The depth of our relationship with Him will determine the strength of spiritual direction. The greater our obedience to God, the smaller the chances for spiritual distress.

Although we speak of the necessity for physical restoration, emotional reeducation and/or spiritual regeneration, every disorder—whatever its origin—is a disorder of the whole person. Depression is not only a multifaceted and complex disorder, but it is an interactional and self-sustaining disorder. Physical, psychological, and spiritual factors act and feed on one another. In every case of depression, both in origin and expression, there is involvement of the entire person. (Brandt, *Victory Over Depression*, Baker Book House, 1988)

The Emotion of Joy
Now that we have taken a look at anger, anxiety, and depression, we are probably more than ready to reflect for a few moments on the last one of our four basic emotions: the emotion of *joy*. The very word *joy* evokes a good feeling within us and is a reminder of the incredible power of thoughts. Joy, as in the case of anger, anxiety, or depression, is not something that just happens. It does not fall on us out of a "joy-tree," it does not jump off some joyful person, and it does not automatically result from specific joyful facts or events in our lives.

Joy, like any other emotive feeling, results from our perceptions (conscious awareness of something) and self-talk (words, thoughts, beliefs), about real or perceived joyful events. If we love a cherry blossom tree in bloom, we might indeed experience a great feeling of joy as we walk under that tree, and its fragrant blossoms gently drift on our shoulders. But guess what! We may also experience a great feeling of joy when we are at home and simply *see* a picture of that tree in our mind's eye and *think* joyful thoughts about this scene.

We Must Focus on God for a Happy Emotional Life

It is a simple, but powerful fact that most individuals can literally choose how they want to feel. Obviously, it may be difficult to make ourselves feel good (or even calm) when we are undergoing tremendous hardships or prolonged physical pain. Yet, wherever we look, we find individuals who are joyful, even under very challenging conditions. When it comes to our emotional life, one thing is for sure: We cannot have positive *and* negative feelings at the same time. If we want to overcome unhappiness, we must focus on happy facts and events. Surely, there is no better way to do this than to focus on the wonderful nature of God Himself and the manifold gifts He so richly bestows on us, His children. Whatever the sources, or causes, of our unhappiness, we best look to God for help and reorientation. We must take God's promises seriously, and fully believe that He will ". . . give good gifts to those who ask Him" (Matt. 7:11).

God has provided us with such useful emotional experiences as anger, sadness, restlessness, and gladness. But aggressive anger, depressive illness, anxiety disorders, or mania, are not useful; God clearly wants to help us deal with them.

Mercy and Responsibility

God made us "players" in all areas of human life. Throughout the Scriptures, we are confronted with the necessity to choose wisely. Moses, thousands of years ago, understood the impact of choice: "This day I call heaven and earth as witnesses against you that I have set before you life and death, blessings and curses. Now choose life, so that you and your children may live . . ." (Deut. 30:19).

The most powerful psychotherapeutic method in use today is *cognitive therapy*. Here individuals are taught how they can rethink and replace, self-defeating thoughts, beliefs, and attitudes. Some individuals erroneously believe that this is a modern thera-

Understanding Our Emotions

peutic approach. Its roots, however, lie solidly in both the Old and New Testament. This book, *The Renewed Mind*, and its two companion volumes, *The Consistent Overcomer*, and *The Loving Soul*, contain many of the principles of *Christian Cognitive Therapy* which, by the grace of God, I have successfully used for the past two decades.

Joyfully, we can attest to God's marvelous provision for us: freedom from bondage, be it mental, emotional, or spiritual. No one sums this up more eloquently than the beloved apostle Paul: "For you did not receive a spirit that makes you a slave again to fear, but you received the Spirit of sonship. And by him we cry, *Abba*, Father. The Spirit himself testifies that we are God's children. Now if we are children, then we are heirs—heirs of God and co-heirs with Christ . . . ." (Rom. 8:15–17).

The Spirit of adoption is the spirit of freedom from bondage—the privilege of every member of God's household who makes right choices. God, blessedly, is our ally in overcoming destructive emotions. He wants us to have victory over the things of this world (1 John 4:4); joy—even in various trials (1 Pet. 1:6); freedom from despair, even in the midst of perplexity (2 Cor. 4:8); the privilege of casting our anxieties on Him (1 Pet. 5:7); soundness of body, mind, and spirit (1 Thess. 5:23); and the benefits go on and on! These scriptures, and so many more, remind us that we are not robots, or victims of forces beyond our control. We have been graced with mercy and responsibility. We are privileged participants in the arena of life. We have choices to make, commitments to pursue, and a tremendous say in the kind of emotions that can fill our hearts and minds.

Let us be truly committed to think and speak right; to live a life filled with the joy of the Lord. Let's be ready to let our light shine and share with others our many blessings. To best accomplish these things, we need to be as healthy as possible—physically, mentally, and spiritually: "May your whole spirit, soul and body be kept blameless at the coming of our Lord Jesus Christ. The one who calls you is faithful and he will do it" (1 Thess. 5:23,24).

7

Making Sound Decisions

"Present your case," says the LORD. "Set forth your arguments...."
—Isa. 41:21

Presenting our case to others is not always easy. At times, it is very hard to convince other persons that we really have done our homework and have very good reasons for the decisions we have made. Some individuals may insist that we explain our reasons (Isa. 41:21), explain things in detail, and be prepared to defend our choices or point of view. In our personal life, however, there may not be anyone who challenges us to carefully check on the many decisions we continually make. How can we be sure that we are making the best possible decisions?

Steps to Sound Decision Making

Sound decisions must be factual and reasonable, but, hopefully, they are also *positive*. To make sure that our decisions are sound, we simply ask: "Is my decision realistic, rational, and positive?" Let's look at these three questions.

Is My Decision Realistic?

This is the first, and also the most important question to ask. If our decisions are not factual—not in line with objective reality, for example, the Word of God—then it is unlikely that we are making sound decisions. Ask questions such as these: "Is my decision based on scripture?" "Is it in harmony with the will of God?" "Can it be verified by others?" "Is it concrete, practical, real?" "Is it nonspeculative?" "Is it based on fact and not on assumptions?" If the decision is a realistic one, then, and only then, proceed to the next question.

Is My Decision Rational?

Reasonable decisions help us to achieve our goals. These goals may pertain to our family life, career, or general well-being (physical, emotional, and spiritual), but no goal is more important than spiritual achievement. We are to use our talents, not merely to improve our life here on earth, but to serve God as best we can. The latter may include being a good disciple, witness, or friend, and by participating in social programs that further the well-being of others.

Is My Decision Positive?

Positive decisions are confident, definite, expectant, hopeful, optimistic, and sure; rather than doubtful, lukewarm, negative, or pessimistic.

The Limitations of Objective Reality

Ideally, all of our decisions are factual and reasonable, as well as optimistic. It is unlikely, however, that this is always possible. Whatever the situation may be, it is very important that our decisions are based on objective reality—that they are as factual and honest as possible. Nevertheless, there is no escaping the fact that human beings are—and will remain—fallible, imperfect, and sinful. The Scriptures gently remind us not to be "wise in our own eyes" (Prov. 3:7). The advice is also clear: We must look to God for guidance in all that we do. Even so, the question must be asked—can Christians really be objective?

Jesus said, ". . . you will know the truth, and the truth will set you free" (John 8:32). First, we need to understand the truth about ourselves, namely that we are lost sinners without direction, lost without God. Once we recognize that Jesus is the truth (God's answer to all our needs), we are ready to decide for Him, turn to Him, and follow Him. Throughout the Scriptures, we find there is a constant emphasis on the truth—truth based on everlasting objective reality. Or, if you will, truth based on eternal facts, rather than subjective assumptions. Belief in God has brought joy, compassion, wisdom, understanding, patience, knowledge, unending faith, hope, and love to the hearts of people everywhere. Nothing is more objective than the reality of God.

The reality of a loving God, however, is not accepted by everyone. Also, there often is a lot of resistance, or resentment, on the part of those who, sometimes quite justifiably, see Christians as far too absolutistic, dogmatic, or perfectionistic. We must have moderation in all things, be humble, and do our best not to offend anyone. Having said this, it is also important to note that there are no human beings who do not have *some* absolutes, who do not follow *some* dogmatic rules, or have *some* perfectionistic tendencies. Even those who declare that there are no absolutes—there is no truth to religion, and there is no God—are, of course, themselves engaged in absolutism.

Nevertheless, we must remember that we "know in part" and can only be objective within the limits of our genetic, social, intellectual, and emotional capacity. We are sinful creatures, with imperfect knowledge and limited experiences, who live in an imperfect world. It is not at all smart to be engaged in "all-ness" thinking—to think that we have all the answers. Children, as well as very old individuals, or those with organic brain disorders, mental handicaps, nutritional deficiencies, and many such issues, are often more prone to think that they are "all-knowing." As will be shown in a later chapter, there are also individuals whose unhealthy personalities may prevent them from being very objective. We need love

The Renewed Mind

and patience in our dealings with those who are unable to accept their fallibility and imperfections.

The Soundest Decision

The main purpose of this book is to help us overcome physical, mental, emotional, and other limitations that may stand in the way of attaining a renewed mind and transformed life. It will not be possible, however, to even be "in the race" for a renewed mind and transformed life, unless we are members of the household of God.

We cannot be a Christian overcomer without first being a Christian. It is therefore the soundest decision of our life to submit our imperfect will to the perfect will of our Heavenly Father. Once we realize that life without God *is* meaningless, then our motive for wanting to find God has been established, and the process of finding Him may actually already be underway. God wants us to yield to Him: to answer His call. He wants "self" to move over and let Him sit on the throne of our heart. But, God will not crash the gates to the throne room. He wants that place freely offered by a willing servant.

God is a God of knowledge and wisdom. He wants us to make sound decisions based on discernment. In order to make a choice in line with God's intent, we may need to look closely at our situation and observe what this world has to offer—how the followers of the trends of this world fare. Then we may want to turn around and look at the claims that God makes in the gospel and see what happens in the lives of those who trust and follow Jesus. We can know God by hearing His call through His Word. Faith, blessed faith, comes from hearing the Word of God (Rom. 10:17). To believe is to say "amen" to the story of salvation, as it catches up with the stories of our lives.

Once we become acquainted with the Word of God, we will understand that God calls us out of the darkness of a self-centered existence and into the light of communion with Him and other believers. When we listen to His call, and choose in His favor, we can embrace an abundant, eternal, and joyful life. The Scriptures tell us that "God is love" (1 John 4:8), so He naturally wants His children to be well. He wants His sons and daughters to be free from dysfunctional anxieties, fears, depressions, bad habits, loneliness, boredom, anger, frustration, or whatever else troubles them. God wants his children to be healed spiritually, mentally, and physically (Exod. 15:26; Ps. 103:3).

It is urgently important that we investigate the claims made by God. In 1 John 4:6, we read: "We are from God, and whoever knows God listens to us; but whoever is not from God does not listen to us . . ." "But," we might cry out, "then it is impossible for those who do not believe in God ever to hear Him." Not so, for God goes on to explain that by reading His Word (Rom. 10:17) and by loving Him and others, He will dwell in us and will give us His Spirit (1 John 4:13).

God makes it easy for us to know Him by means of a plan known as the "plan of salvation." He has provided a simple plan, whereby we may not only have salvation (the preservation from eternal misery and reception into a state of happiness), but also learn to speak with God, receive the Holy Spirit, and obtain answers to many of our questions. We can test whether or not God will do the things He promises in the Scriptures. Here are the simple steps for the soundest decision we will ever make:

- *We must acknowledge our sins.* Not one of us is perfect; as the Bible reminds us, "For all have sinned, and fall short of the glory of God" (Rom. 3:23). Knowing we are sinners is not enough, however. We must admit this to God and ask for His mercy.
- *We must repent of our sins.* The admission of our sins is just the beginning. We must have true remorse for our transgressions. The Bible tells us ". . . unless you repent, you too will all perish" (Luke:13:3). Only after we repent can we start a new life in Christ.
- *We must confess our sins.* It is all-important that we confess our sins. In 1 John 1:9, we read: "If we confess our sins he is faithful and just and will forgive us our sins,

and purify us from all unrighteousness." Only when we actually confess can we receive the great reward of forgiveness and adoption.
- *We must forsake our sins.* All evil things come out of our heart, and we must accept the good before we can reject the evil. Isaiah 55:7 expresses it this way: "Let the wicked forsake his way and the evil man his thoughts. Let him turn to the LORD, and He will have mercy on him . . . for he will freely pardon."
- *We must believe in Jesus.* We can only act on the thoughts we believe. Only if we believe in Jesus Christ as the Son of God, as the promised Savior, can we have the benefits of His sacrifice or love: "For God so loved the world that he gave his one and only Son, that whoever believes in him shall not perish but have eternal life" (John 3:16).
- *We must receive Jesus into our hearts.* Only when Jesus becomes the center of our lives do we receive His power. John 1:12 says: ". . . to all who received him, to those who believed in his name, he gave the right to become children of God. . . ."
- *We must not overlook baptism.* Although we are saved ". . . by grace . . . through faith" (Eph. 2:8), outward symbolic actions, such as baptism, should not be downplayed. Jesus Himself said in Mark 16:16: "Whoever believes and is baptized will be saved, but whoever does not believe will be condemned." It is through baptism that we are incorporated into the fellowship of believers.

As we can readily see from the straightforward steps that are involved in the plan of salvation, there is *no* arbitrariness in the Christian's choice; it is *not* a blind choice; it is *not* based on blind faith. We become Christians *only* by way of a sound decision—a decision that is based on truth, reason, and faith. We become Christians only after we have rationally decided that God's way is preferable over any other way. As Christians, we make life-enhancing choices. We live our lives with the least possible amount of intrapersonal or interpersonal difficulties and with the greatest amount of truth, reason, faith, and love—all very rational choices!

Whether we make decisions of a spiritual, mental/emotional, or physical nature, we do well to consider the three questions that we looked at in the beginning of this chapter. Choosing to do what is objectively in our best interest, helps us to achieve our dearest goals. It enables us to live peacefully with others, become physically healthier, mentally happier, and spiritually fulfilled. In the next chapter, we will consider how we can use our sound decision making skills to learn new life-enhancing behaviors.

8

LEARNING NEW LIFE-ENHANCING BEHAVIOR

> Therefore, if anyone is in Christ, he is a new creation; the old has gone, the new has come!
> —2 Cor. 5:17

Contrary to what others may have told us, or what we may have told ourselves, it is possible to learn new life-enhancing behavior. We *can* be overcomers. We have God's promise, confirmed by two thousand years of evidence, that fallible, imperfect, and sinful, persons *can* become new creations in Christ. This process, however, requires that we submit ourselves wholeheartedly to the perfect will of God. This in turn means that we must get rid of negative personality traits, selfishness, self-pity, addictions, and other self-defeating or destructive habits. We must learn to focus on what we want, who we would like to be, how we desire to live, and so forth. We must be more solution-focused and less problem-centered.

Becoming Solution-Focused

Our new focus must be on things above and beyond ourselves. Jesus promises us this: "If you remain in me and my words remain

The Renewed Mind

in you, ask whatever you wish, and it will be given you"(John 15:7). How are we to ask? Doubtfully? Fearfully? Say one thing but mean another? Listen again to Jesus: ". . . I tell you that men will have to give account on the day of judgment for every careless word they have spoken. For by your words you will be acquitted, and by your words you will be condemned" (Matt. 12:36,37).

The Scriptures are abundantly clear, and history firmly confirms, that human beings are mainly the end product of their own thoughts and utterances. Victory in life depends not so much on what, where, or who we are, as on how we think. When the apostle Paul cries out, "Do not conform any longer to the pattern of this world, but be transformed by the renewing of your mind." He, too, makes it clear that we, ourselves, are the *cause* of our success or failure—the cause and not the source, because the *source* of our transformation, the source of every good thing in our life, is God. We are standing, as it were, between two forces: good and evil: ". . . I have set before you life and death, blessings and curses. Now choose. . . ." (Deut. 30:19). If we choose life, we must learn to become solution-focused: perceive more clearly, think more constructively, and act more positively. A new life is waiting for us, if we are willing to radically stick to truth, reason, faith, and love.

Learning to Perceive More Clearly

In order to see as accurately as possible, we need objective perceptions. A perception is a stimulus being registered by our brain, but, unlike photographic plates, our brain adds evaluative thoughts to perceptions and creates what is known as apperceptions. The latter are perceptions, plus some meaningful labels that we have attached to them. All too often, those labels are incorrect. Sadly, we are never completely objective and frequently quite unobjective. Not only is it unlikely to have perfect sense organs, it is even more unlikely to use sensory impulses in an unbiased manner: "All a man's ways . . . ," the book of Proverbs reminds us, ". . . seem right to him" (Prov. 21:2). How true! As fallible, imperfect, and sinful human beings, we cannot be completely objective. All we can do is approximate objective reality. These important insights will hopefully compel us to ensure that our perceptions are as accurate as possible. This is what I have said elsewhere (Brandt, 1988) on this subject:

> Once people realize that good thinking leads to good feelings, they are more ready to go for the good thinking. Many, however, never get to that stage because they are bound not only to erroneous thoughts, but also to erroneous perceptions. Take a simple test. Read the statement below, and after having done so, count the number of F's.

> FINISHED FILES ARE THE RESULT OF YEARS OF SCIENTIFIC STUDY COMBINED WITH THE EXPERIENCE OF MANY YEARS.

After counting the F's, go to the end of the chapter to find further information.

Learning to Speak More Constructively

After taking this test, or perhaps administering it to others, we should be more aware of the importance of accurate perceptions and constructive self-talk. Nowhere else is this better stated than in Proverbs 18:21: "The tongue has the power of life and death, and those who love it will eat its fruit." I have seen the devastating power of destructive self-talk in hundreds of individuals who were struggling with various emotional problems, impoverished relationships, poor health, marital discord, and so forth. And I have been blessed to have witnessed how most of these individuals changed their lives by switching to realistic, rational, and positive self-talk. We have thousands of years of documented proof on the power of the tongue. How much more proof do we need? Sadly, for some individuals, no amount of proof will ever be enough, and they will continue to lead unhappy lives.

The Renewed Mind

Self-talk refers to those cognitions (thoughts, beliefs, and attitudes) that are part of our habitual vocabulary. It involves thinking or speaking about real or imaginary facts or events and may consist of automatic reactions to various stimuli. Our self-talk ideally focuses on the things we want; we are to look forward not backward: "And be constantly renewed in the spirit of the mind (having a fresh mental and spiritual attitude), and put on the new man created in God's image (Godlike) in true righteousness and holiness" (Eph. 4:22 AMP). Specific self-talk (specific use of the tongue) results in specific feelings. The following are some examples of self-talk and the resulting feelings of anger, anxiety, depression, and guilt:

They must shut up.	I am a big loser.	I believe I will be hurt.	I shouldn't have.
He must apologize.	Nobody loves me.	Everything is going wrong.	It's all my fault.
She ought to know.	I am worthless.	I am afraid of what's next.	I am a bad person.
Anger	Depression	Anxiety	Guilt

The Seven Steps of Learning New Behaviors

Intellectual Insight

Unless we recognize our troublesome behavior, we are unlikely to change it. As a rule, we only change a behavior if we believe it is worthwhile to do so. Before we can get to this point, we must be aware that something is amiss; we need intellectual insight. Many persons, however, have self-defeating or self-destructive behaviors without fully understanding this. If we are unaware, for example, that tobacco kills more than three hundred thousand persons annually in this country, and perhaps millions of persons throughout the world (five hundred thousand in Europe alone), then we are less likely to stop the danger-

Learning New Life-Enhancing Behavior

ous practice of tobacco smoking. On the other hand, if we do know these statistics, but we *assume* that smoking will not harm us, we still lack intellectual insight and are unlikely to change our smoking behavior. If we have intellectual insight, we recognize that we have a problem and that a solution is possible.

STRONG DESIRE

It is obvious that few, if any, independent, and otherwise capable, adults are going to change their behavior unless they want to do this. Even if they believe that a problem can be resolved, they may still not do anything about it. Perhaps they see it as too much work, fear that they could fail, or have some other reason. Personal change requires motivation: A strong desire to gain something or get away from something. Even individuals with serious handicaps or limitations can be overcomers when they have both insight and motivation.

Consider Helen Keller, who was both blind and deaf since early infancy. "One can never," said Helen Keller, "consent to creep when one feels an impulse to soar." And, listen to her again: "The joy of surmounting obstacles which once seemed unremoveable and pushing the frontier of accomplishment further—what joy is there like unto it?" Some may think that Helen Keller was just a rare exception in this world and that it is very unrealistic to think that seriously handicapped individuals can be true overcomers. Not so! Anyone who can understand the contents of this book can surmount obstacles, soar higher, and reach new goals in this life.

There are millions of handicapped overcomers in this world. Take, for example, Joel Sonnenberg, who, at the time of this writing, is a student at Taylor University in Indiana. He is a friendly, happy, hopeful, kind, merciful, and outgoing young man. He enjoys sports, has an active life, loves people, and has a very strong faith. Joel Sonnenberg is a great inspiration to all who meet him or who know the story of his life. When he was twenty-two months old, Joel Sonnenberg received third, fourth, and fifth degree burns to over eighty-eight percent of his body. Given only a 10 percent chance to live, he has, over a period of many years, endured nearly

The Renewed Mind

fifty operations. He has no hair or eyebrows—the least of his troubles—no left hand, and a right hand with pincers rather than fingers. Outwardly scarred, but inwardly very beautiful, this young man clearly lives by truth, reason, faith, and love. He is a true example of an overcomer, a person with a winning attitude, who, in the pursuit of a wholesome goal, always gets up one more time, every time. Overcomers, of course, need more than just insight and desire. They must be willing to work: "Do not merely listen to the word," we read in James 1:22, "and so deceive yourselves. Do what it says." Doing is what the next two steps are all about.

Vicarious Practice

Mental practice is often just as important as actual practice when it comes to changing old behaviors into new ones. It may not matter which kind of practice we start with—actual or mental—but it does matter that we practice correctly. Many, if not most, of our troubles are the result of doing things incorrectly. We are often steeped in unrealistic, irrational, or negative thoughts, which produce inappropriate feelings of anger, anxiousness, sadness, and so forth.

Without correct practice, we cannot overcome our problems. The key to learning new life-enhancing behavior is found in the consistent practice of our newly-desired thoughts, traits, feelings, and behaviors. A safe effective way to learn a new behavior is through mental practice. Mental practice, also known as vicarious practice, simply means that we mentally see and hear ourselves behaving in wholesome, constructive, and God-honoring ways. After we have prayed, and are as calm as possible, we can spend some quiet time with our eyes closed, mentally rehearsing some newly-desired behavior. We can also write a complete script and commit it to memory, or we can make a tape recording of this script.

Some individuals are hesitant, or reluctant, to engage in planned mental practice. Perhaps they do not realize that *all* human beings continuously engage in mental practice but that only a few seem to do it in a systematic and constructive way. In sports, vicarious practice is a common occurrence. Athletes know that

Learning New Life-Enhancing Behavior

good mental practice, as well as actual practice, can make the difference between a champion and a nonchampion. When we practice our new behavior long enough, this behavior will become habitual. In fact, once this happens, the reeducation process has been completed. Regrettably, many individuals do not have an opportunity to get enough safe, actual practice to learn newly desired behaviors. The answer to that difficulty, however, is found in doing correct mental practice.

In mental practice, we see a "movie" in our mind of a situation where we experience a newly desired behavior. By repeatedly doing this, we train our brain to spontaneously react, or respond, in this way in an actual situation. Consider this example: A supervisor with a fear of public speaking has been asked to give a presentation to a group of salespersons at work. The presentation is due in three weeks. Although a rehearsal would help, there is no group of volunteers to practice on. The supervisor is increasingly worried about the event, and after one week, finds herself more and more nervous. Even if she does not realize it, she has been doing some irrational mental practice, seeing herself stuttering and feeling foolish in front of the sales staff. She is losing sleep, not eating well, and doing poorly on her job. After one week of going "downhill," she hears about mental practice. Desperate to try anything, she works out the following script:

> It is 9 A.M., and I am entering the conference room where the sales staff is waiting to hear my presentation on customer services. I know the subject very well, have committed my talk to memory, and also have a 3x5 card with six main points. This will help me to stay on track, and refresh my memory, if necessary. I notice the clock on the wall that states the time as nine o'clock. I am happy to see that all is going according to schedule. I smile as I look at the familiar faces of the sales staff. I hear myself saying "Good morning," while looking directly at the face of the chairperson.
>
> I walk over to the speaker's rostrum and place the card in the right-hand corner, where I can easily spot it. I am aware that I know most of the persons on the sales staff and remind myself

that this is an excellent chance to share details on customer service with them. As soon as I have placed the card on the rostrum, I start to speak. I make no jokes or personal statements. I begin immediately by reminding the sales staff of the excellent record the company has in customer service and how this has helped the sales staff deal confidently with their clients. After covering the first item on my card, I take a quick look at all of their faces, and, within a few seconds, I am speaking on the second item. I confidently cover each point. The clock clearly shows that it is 9:10 A.M., and I have used my allotted time. The presentation was a success, the staff seemed pleased, I thank them for what they are doing for my department and the company and wish them a happy day. I give a big smile to the chairperson and hear myself saying "Thank you for inviting me to your meeting this morning." The time on the clock shows it is 9:11 A.M.

There are all kinds of variations that can be made to this script. It can be more or less detailed; it can even include the entire talk. Hopefully the supervisor made a tape recording of her talk and listened to it many times before giving her speech. Here, in any case, is an example of safe and effective practice. It would have been difficult to ask a surrogate sales staff to listen to her speech twenty or thirty times, but practicing vicariously was an easy thing to do. We can make mental practice scripts on just about any subject we wish, from not overeating, to not arguing with difficult persons.

How often should we do a mental practice exercise? There are no scientific rules on this, but a few times a day over a period of one or two weeks will prove effective in many cases. Whatever we do, we must not get lost in theories or technicalities. Many educational systems fail because they are unnecessarily complicated. We can have the behaviors we desire, if we repeatedly first do them in our imagination and then in actual practice.

ACTUAL PRACTICE

Actual practice is obviously very important. The proverbial proof of the pudding is in the eating, and the proof of having successfully mastered a new life-enhancing behavior is in doing the actual behavior. Once we have practiced vicariously, we need to do so in actuality. In order to do this, we may have to search for opportunities to practice our newly desired behavior of remaining calm, caring, and constructive. Here, once again, we need to remind ourselves that our practice is to reflect truth, reason, and faith. Ultimately this will translate into seeking guidance from the Holy Spirit—the Spirit of truth and love. If we think well, we love well and act well.

Overcoming Dissonance

In the process of overcoming self-defeating behavior, we may experience what is known as cognitive-emotive dissonance—disharmony between the thinking and feeling portions of our brain. We may know we are doing things right, but it feels wrong. We know, for example, that it is right to stay calm with an overly demanding person, but it does not feel right. Let us look at another example of mental-emotive dissonance: Traveling in England, we know it is correct to drive on the left side of the road, but for Americans who are used to driving on the right-hand side of the road, it just does not feel right. What are we to do? We simply acknowledge the feeling and continue to do what we know is right. The same rule applies to dealing with an overly demanding person. Continue to do what is right, and, sooner or later, our thoughts and feelings will become congruent. We must stick to our thoughts and not our feelings. If in doubt, we always travel by our compass.

Emotional Insight

Emotional insight does not require any effort on our part. Having emotional insight, however, is very important, for it encourages us to go on doing what we are doing. It is a reminder that we are right on target—we know that we are doing things right, and it also feels right (to not be angry, to not overeat, and so forth).

Embracing New Behavior

If we keep on practicing our new behavior, we suddenly discover that this behavior is no longer new for us. We no longer consciously think about the desired behavior; it has become a normal occurrence, an automatic event. We thank God, happily embrace our new attitude, habit, or personality trait, and go on with life!

From this chapter, we learn that God loves us and helps us to be overcomers in Christ. As long as we look to the Holy Spirit as our Guide, we will get to our destination safely. The more joyfully we submit ourselves to the perfect will of God, the more we discover that it is essential to see clearly and speak constructively. With *insight, desire,* and *consistent practice,* we eventually learn new life-enhancing behaviors. All our habits—good or bad—have been learned through repetition. If we want new behaviors, we must stop concentrating on our old habits and problems. Whenever we think or talk about them, analyze or dissect them, condemn or justify them, we will keep them alive! Instead, we must lay claim to the Word of God: ". . . I have set before you life and death, blessings and curses. Now choose . . ." (Deut. 30:19). We must use the power of the mind wisely, for in so doing we have "the power of life." And that is a fact!

NOTE: The Mini-Perception Test. Most individuals count only three F's. The correct answer, however, is six F's. If you found only three, you probably missed the three *of* words. I was given this test at a conference in England in 1979 and have no idea about its origin.

Part Four:

A Sound Mind in a Sound Body

9

EMOTIONAL PROBLEMS MAY HAVE A PHYSICAL BASIS

> Therefore, I urge you, brothers, in view of God's mercy, to offer your bodies as living sacrifices, holy and pleasing to God—this is your spiritual act of worship.
> —Rom. 12:1

When it comes to our mental health, we frequently overlook the very important role our physical health plays. We have a tendency to forget that sometimes our bouts with anger, anxiety, depression, restlessness, sleeplessness, or a host of other problems, may have their primary source in a disturbed body chemistry. It is difficult, and sometimes impossible, to think right, or to feel right, with a brain that is deficient in glucose, serotonin, or some other brain chemical. The reverse, of course, also holds true. When our minds are sufficiently disturbed, our body chemistry will also be disturbed. We are all too familiar with the many stress-related illnesses that plague millions of individuals. Body and mind are interdependent; we have no convenient zippers between them. What affects the one will affect the other.

The main purpose of this chapter is to make us more aware that a sound mind requires a sound body, and vice versa. All too many individuals are "spinning their wheels," trying to have a happy emotional, social, or even spiritual life, while ignoring the crucial role of body chemistry in these events. There is perhaps far more at stake than we may realize. To think that a healthy personality, renewed mind, and transformed life, are directly related to a well-functioning electrochemical brain, may seem rather far-fetched, yet it is an undeniable fact. The mind consists of functional elements of the brain, and the latter is wholly dependent on the body. If we ignore our bodies, we also ignore our minds.

A Healthy Brain Needs a Healthy Body
Good thinking depends on a well-functioning mind, and, in turn, on a well-functioning brain. Our brain works hard, even while we are sleeping, and consumes a great amount of energy. Its need for glucose is greater than that of any other organ in the body. The main fuel for our billions of brain cells consists of oxygen, glucose, amino acids, fatty acids, and vitamins. In addition, there are other brain chemicals, such as acetylcholine, dopamine, norepinephrine, and serotonin, that function as chemical messengers between brain cells. *All brain chemicals—fuel and messengers—depend on a well-nourished and well-maintained body.* In addition to a steady and sufficient supply of healthy nutrients, the brain also needs rest, relaxation, and stimulation for optimum functioning.

The Scriptures, although not a handbook on nutrition, provide us with general guidelines for a healthy and sensible lifestyle. From the Bible we learn that we are created in God's image; that our body is the temple of the Holy Spirit, and must be presented as a "living sacrifice" in which God is to be magnified (Gen. 1:26,27; 1 Cor. 6:19; Rom. 12:1; Phil. 1:20). This is not something we can quietly overlook. It is sad to say, however, that all too often, we ignore God's advice and keep on believing that all illnesses that befall us are normal, natural, or unpreventable. This belief is incorrect. The overwhelming majority of all physical and emotional problems are the direct result of unrealistic, irrational, and other-

Emotional Problems May Have a Physical Basis

wise unacceptable lifestyles. Unacceptable, we must assume, to a God of wisdom and infinite knowledge; a God who seeks to heal and not destroy; a God who builds up and does not tear down. Is it not utterly foolish to ask God for health and strength with the same mouth by which we are making ourselves sick?

Modern research and day-to-day observations confirm that our most serious health threats come from chronic illnesses. It is also our most costly national problem. Seven out of ten leading causes of death are directly related to the behavioral choices we make, such as choices in sexual behavior, smoking, drinking alcohol, the use of drugs (legal and illegal), and so forth. Excessive stress also plays a major role in our declining health, but happily, we have plenty of information available on how to reduce stress. Some illnesses are related to genetics and some are nearly impossible to prevent, yet from 75 to 85 percent of our physical and emotional problems are preventable. Most of our physical and emotional problems are the result of self-defeating and self-destructive lifestyles.

Nevertheless, it is also true that some individuals may unwittingly find themselves in disease-producing social or physical environments. Few individuals, for example, have access to the statistical data that identifies which regions in our states and country have higher disease rates than elsewhere. We need a lot of discernment in this regard. Our health is not something to be taken for granted; nor can we unquestioningly leave matters pertaining to our health in the hands of strangers. We ourselves must actively guard it!

Unhealthy Lifestyles Produce Unhealthy Bodies

Most of us are aware of the well-known risk factors that may lead to serious illness and early death. Nevertheless, it is probably a good idea to have another thorough look at them. Consider the following about the leading killers in our midst:

- Cancer is often the direct result of *improper diet,* the use of *alcohol* and *tobacco products,* and *environmental factors.*
- Cerebrovascular disease is related to the use of *tobacco,* the excessive intake of *cholesterol* in our diet, *elevated blood*

pressure (which may have many sources, including stress), and/or a *sedentary lifestyle*.
- Chronic lung disease results mainly from *tobacco products* and *environmental pollution*, including the exposure of innocent people to so-called second-hand smoke.
- Heart disease has been directly linked to *tobacco use, obesity, high cholesterol levels*, and a *sedentary lifestyle*.

As we look at the foregoing paragraph, we find that tobacco, improper diet, alcohol, and a sedentary lifestyle play a role in the four leading causes of illness and early death. Yet, all four of these causes are preventable. There seems to be increasing evidence that lack of information, lack of wisdom, and lack of motivation are behind our failure to stop the suffering and early demise of millions of individuals. We might conclude that many of our health problems are due to ignorance (we don't know any better), stupidity (we don't care about ourselves), meanness (we don't care about others), and/or powerful addictions, if we are dependent on alcohol, nicotine, and other substances.

In spite of overwhelming scientific evidence, we find that many individuals still do not realize that most illnesses are preventable. One in two persons in this country dies before his or her time! We must stop blaming all untimely deaths on the will of God. It is not God who is "calling us home," but our use of alcohol, tobacco, junk food, and other aspects of death-defying lifestyles. Imagine how far we have strayed from having "dominion over the earth," when inanimate objects have "irresistible" powers over us. How can a pack of cigarettes, a can of beer, a donut, or a candy bar be more powerful than a mind under the executive control of the Holy Spirit? How can Christian believers remain in bondage to material things? Are we confused, or are we dishonest with ourselves? Do we claim inability rather than unwillingness? We are a nation of substance junkies—Christians and non-Christians alike. Let's stop bickering over which addictions are worse—neither caffeine addicts nor sugar junkies are in a position to throw stones at those who are addicted to alcohol or drugs. An addiction is an

Emotional Problems May Have a Physical Basis

addiction. This is not pleasing to God, is bad for our physical health, and an obstacle to our emotional and spiritual well-being.

The United States presently has the most overweight population in the world. Nearly one-fourth of our population is obese, and more than half of our population is overweight. How sad that a nation with the most advanced technologies in the world cannot protect its citizens from being strangled by fat. Our national problem with excessive weight can be resolved. Although there are many claims as to its causes (ranging from fat cells, gender, stretched stomachs, glucose disturbances, addictions, allergies, genetics, and brain chemicals), excessive weight remains, more than anything else, a lifestyle problem (Brandt, 1978). It is not due to some genetic disadvantage endured by our citizens, or some disturbed brain chemistry primarily found in our country (and increasingly in affluent western Europe), it is mainly due to our excessive caloric intake (especially refined carbohydrates), and our inadequate caloric output.

The answer to lifestyle problems is not found in making excuses or calling bad habits medical problems. The answer lies in wisdom, knowledge, self-control, and self-denial. This can be painful and may entail personal sacrifice. If more individuals understood what is at stake, more might be willing to develop healthier lifestyles.

A partial answer may well be found in improved education. Well-informed and educated individuals are more likely to make wise choices. It has been said that those who have more than a high school education are healthier and live longer than those who have less than a high school education. We could blame this on economic and other factors, but there is undoubtedly also an important relationship with sound decision making. In a cross-cultural study on self-defeating beliefs (Brandt, 1978), I found that better educated persons held fewer self-defeating beliefs than less well-educated persons. I also found that women, especially college-educated women, held fewer self-defeating beliefs than men with a similar education. The reason that women outlive men is perhaps more influenced by sound decision-making and healthier lifestyles than genetics.

The Principle Reasons for Poor Health

To appreciate the impact of lifestyle on health and longevity, we simply need to remember that the four leading contributors to early death in this country are poor diet, tobacco use, alcohol use, and lack of exercise. These factors play a far greater role in mortality rates than accidents or infectious agents, yet it is the latter that receives primary attention from health officials. It goes well beyond the scope of this book to consider this subject in-depth, yet it seems prudent to at least briefly look at some common destructive habits.

Poor Diet

Overeating, our national pastime, has created a nation where the majority of our citizens are overweight. Abnormalities in metabolism sometimes leads to the uncontrolled storage of fat, but most of the time problems with excess weight are lifestyle problems—a lifestyle that is often dominated by lack of knowledge. In the meantime, excessive body fat is not so much an aesthetic problem as a health problem. We pay far too much attention to the outside of the body and not nearly enough to the inside.

It is the interior of our bodies that tells the real story—with villains like coronary artery disease, diabetes, gall bladder disease, and hypertension. Obesity, one of the leading causes of hypertension, plays a role in *angina pectoris* (strangling of the chest) where the heart muscle receives an insufficient supply of blood. Fatty deposits in the arteries, layers of fat around the heart, excessive deposits of fat in the liver cells, and the smothering of the kidneys with large deposits of fat tissue, are only some aspects of this unpleasant and dangerous problem—dangerous enough to result in a far higher mortality rate for those who are overweight. In fact, the mortality rate is twice as high for those who are 40 percent overweight, than those who are not overweight.

Emotional Problems May Have a Physical Basis

Many reams of paper have been written on the dangers of our national eating habits, but most individuals continue to ignore warning after warning. How much research, how many government papers, and how many physical warning signs are we waiting for? The proof is obtained easily enough. Let us just *not* eat the pudding! Faulty nutrition, whether from incomplete assimilation, poor diet, or overeating, is an even greater killer than alcohol and tobacco combined, but because of its insidious nature, we easily overlook this.

Tobacco use

The information on tobacco and its destructive effects is so well known that it may seem unnecessary to belabor this point. We do well, however, to keep in mind that nicotine and other tobacco substances are real killers. It is difficult to imagine that worldwide, perhaps millions of individuals die annually because of tobacco use. The use of tobacco products is a leading cause of disease and death, and is often responsible for emphysema, lung disease, mouth cancer, hypoglycemia, circulatory problems, and lack of resistance to viruses, to name just a few.

Alcohol use

Another killer in our midst is alcohol. Its incredibly destructive nature sometimes gets overshadowed by news of some allegedly redeeming quality. Recently, for example, there was confusing publicity about so-called moderate use of alcohol. This may have left the impression that alcohol in small quantities is not only safe, but that it might include a "health benefit." This particular benefit, however, may be obtained merely by drinking nonfermented concord grape juice. There are zero health benefits in any alcoholic drink that can begin to offset the amount of disease and death caused by it. The debate about "safe" drinking and its supposed health benefits is far from new. It has been going on for a very long time—since the fifteenth century!

Some Physical Aspects of Emotional Problems

PHYSICAL ASPECTS OF ANGER

There are many physical conditions that can make us more vulnerable to dysfunctional anger, anxiety, or depression. The many conditions that may arouse anger are truly multifaceted, but whatever its source, anger problems must be resolved at emotional, physical, and spiritual levels.

Anger responses, while involving anger-specific self-talk, are often triggered by certain neurological disorders, hormonal imbalances, nutritional deficiencies, and illnesses such as rheumatoid arthritis. The most common factor, however, and perhaps the most overlooked one, is found in glucose disturbances. Not only high blood sugar levels, but especially low blood sugar levels, make many individuals very susceptible to irritability and anger. Low blood sugar, already a major obstacle to good brain functioning, is also associated with increased levels of epinephrine and cortisol. These substances exacerbate already existing excitability and irritability and make us even more prone to emotional outbursts. Low blood sugar plays such a major role in many emotional difficulties, that we will look at this subject in some detail later in this chapter.

PHYSICAL ASPECTS OF ANXIETY

Anxiety, while involving anxiety-specific self-talk, is more readily found in individuals with certain physical vulnerabilities. For example, some individuals are so sensitive to caffeine that even one cup of coffee may make them more prone to problems with anxiety. There are at least fifty physical sources that may contribute to anxiety. We can broadly divide these sources into *neurological problems* (e.g., migraines or multiple sclerosis); *systemic disorders* (e.g., cardiovascular disease or anemia); *endocrine disturbances* (e.g., thyroid or adrenal dysfunction); *inflammatory disease* (e.g., lupus or rheumatoid arthritis); *toxic conditions* (e.g., amphetamine or caffeine sensitivities); *allergic reactions* (e.g., environmental pollutants or food sensitivities); *nutritional factors* (e.g. vitamin or mineral deficiencies); and scores of other physical sources. Obviously, anxiety, or any other emotional problem, is not always completely self-induced—is not always just "a choice." There are many physical sources for anxiety, as well as a possible genetic predisposition, for those who have a Generalized Anxiety Disorder.

PHYSICAL ASPECTS OF DEPRESSION

The three root sources for depression are a self-destructive lifestyle, self-defeating thinking, and self-alienation from God. In the case of *depressive illness,* however, we may possibly find that genetic factors are at its root. The difference between depression, depressive illness, and a depressive personality have been discussed earlier (in chapter 6), and we need not repeat this here. Any mood disorder, however, may have various underlying physical sources, including illnesses, heredity, endocrine disturbances (e.g., low blood sugar), and malnutrition. A physical examination is always an essential preliminary step in the treatment of emotional problems. Ultimately, of course, any disorder—physical, emotional, or spiritual—is a disorder of the total person. The ideal treatment involves body, mind, and spirit!

Low Blood Sugar: A Common Problem

It is perhaps a good idea to close this chapter with some information on *hypoglycemia*—low blood sugar. While it is only one of numerous physical sources that may play a direct role in our emotional difficulties, it is, in my opinion, one of the most common ones. Regrettably, hypoglycemia is often overlooked, or even rejected, as a possible source for emotional problems by much of the medical profession. There are several reasons for this, but, as one who has dealt with this subject for about twenty-five years, I know there are very few good ones.

I certainly believe it is a major mistake to think of hypoglycemia as inconsequential. Here, for example, is a quote from the highly respected *Textbook of Psychiatry* by Kaplan and Sadock (1985), "If (hypoglycemia) attacks have been severe, prolonged, and recurrent over a long period of time, brain damage may result and lead to long-term changes in personality, severe enough sometimes to resemble chronic schizophrenia, depression, or dementia." This, however, is a very mild and careful statement by conservative physicians. There is a lot more to the story.

Individuals with chronic functional hypoglycemia are prone to get into emotional trouble. For those individuals, even *a little bit* of fasting, strenuous exercise, sleep deprivation, junk food, worry, inappropriate food or drink (such as a cup of regular coffee, a glass of beer or grape juice), or overwork, may be enough to push them "over the edge." This does not always happen right away. Especially if a person's low blood sugar has been arrested, it may seem, for a while at least, that he or she is "normal" like the rest of the world, and, once again, they return to an unhealthy lifestyle. This may go on for weeks, or even months, but the old problem will return with a vengeance. At first it may take two or more stressful events to have a hypoglycemic person "lose it." For example, if the "ex-sufferer" stays up too late, then skips breakfast (or eats a refined carbohydrate breakfast), there may be some very unpleasant physical and/or emotional symptoms. If this is not corrected, then this person will soon be back in low blood sugar "never-never land"—a land of confusion and never-ending unhappy surprises.

In the medical world, hypoglycemia is a designation usually reserved for excessively low levels of glucose in the blood stream. However, excessively low (<60 mg/dl), moderately low (60–70 mg/dl), or slightly low (71–79 mg/dl) blood sugar levels in a nonpregnant and otherwise healthy adult below the age of 50, may not be the ultimate diagnostic criterion. The diagnosis of hypoglycemia is based on both physical *and* mental/emotional symptoms, which cannot be accounted for in other ways, and is substantiated by an Oral Glucose Tolerance Test, or otherwise verified (for example, with nutritional manipulation or other lifestyle variables). Before we discuss the OGTT and some of the common symptoms of low blood sugar, let's take a quick look at two quite different categories of this physical phenomenon.

Emotional Problems May Have a Physical Basis

Two Types of Low Blood Sugar

Functional Hypoglycemia

The most common type of low blood sugar is functional hypoglycemia. There is often no directly identifiable organic disorder underlying this condition. We find something that is dysfunctional rather than a disorder. Functional low blood sugar is believed to be related to lifestyle factors, such as over-consumption of refined carbohydrates (especially sugar and white flour products); the use of caffeine, nicotine, or alcohol; lack of sleep; excessive work; strenuous exercise, or other stressful conditions; a genetic predisposition; and/or an overly sensitive pancreas. The current American diet is seen as a major source of functional hypoglycemia, as well as a source of many serious illnesses. Functional hypoglycemia usually consists of an overreaction by the pancreas to glucose in the bloodstream; an overly sensitive pancreas produces too much insulin and hypoglycemia is the final outcome. Millions of individuals in this country are suffering with functional hypoglycemia, but many of them are unaware that this very treatable condition might be a primary or coexisting source of their emotional or physical problems. Because the excessive consumption of refined carbohydrates may lead to an overload of glucose in the bloodstream and, in turn, excessive insulin production, this condition is often referred to as hyperinsulinism.

Functional hypoglycemia may also result when a person takes drugs that utilize a great deal of glucose, or those that interfere with glucose production, such as alcohol and aspirin. Other reasons for functional hypoglycemia include the removal of all or most of the stomach (postgastrectomy) and inhibition of glucose output due to problems with fructose (hereditary fructose intolerance).

Organic Hypoglycemia

An entirely different story is organic hypoglycemia. Sources for organic hypoglycemia include insulinomas (pancreatic tumors of the beta cells of the islands of Langerhans), which are usually benign; a deficiency of contrainsulin hormones, such as cortisol, glucagon (a polypeptide hormone secreted by the pancreas that stimulates the conversion of glycogen into glucose), growth hormone, epinephrine (adrenaline), and thyroid hormones; or an overdosage of insulin by a diabetic person.

Additional sources of organic hypoglycemia that may lead to excessive glucose utilization (burning up too much sugar) includes: fever (infectious diseases), pregnancy, and large tumors (e.g., sarcomas). Organic hypoglycemia may also result from deficient glucose production due to liver disease; hepatic enzyme defects (enzymes are necessary to convert glycogen—a carbohydrate which is stored mainly in the liver and secondarily in the muscles—into blood sugar); and pituitary, thyroid, or adrenal insufficiency. The latter, in turn, may result from physical, mental, or emotional stressors (including toxins, excessive exercise, overwork and chronic problems with anger, anxiety, or depression). Here we may find an overlap of functional and organic hypoglycemia. There are indeed many sources of hypoglycemia. It is a troublesome condition which always warrants full medical investigation.

Signs and Symptoms of Low Blood Sugar

There are so many physical reasons for low blood sugar problems that it is no wonder that there are also many corresponding or coexisting physical, mental, or emotional signs and symptoms. The more common symptoms, in alphabetical order, include: aching eye sockets, alcohol addiction, anger, anxiousness or anxiety, blackouts, blurred vision, cold extremities, concentration problems, crying or weepiness without specific reason, depression, digestive problems, disturbing dreams or all-out nightmares, dizziness, drowsiness, exhaustion, faintness, forgetfulness, headaches, heart palpitations, hives, inability to go to sleep or go back to sleep, inability to handle pressure, inability to make decisions, irritability, itching skin, lack of initiative, lack of self-control, lack of sexual desire, leg cramps, midmorning or mid-afternoon headaches, cravings (for caffeine, nicotine, or sweets), mental confusion, mood swings, muscle pain, narcolepsy (abnormal attacks of sleepiness,

Emotional Problems May Have a Physical Basis

often in the middle of the day), numbness, nervousness, nicotine addiction, overweight, phobias, rapid pulse, rhinitis, sensitivity to light and/or noise, seizures that cannot be explained, sleepiness after meals, sighing, sinusitis, stomach cramps or uneasiness, sugar addiction, temper tantrums, tremors, ticks or muscle spasms, tiredness, twitching of eyelids, visual disturbances, worrying excessively, and yawning without identifiable cause.

It is, of course, very easy to be skeptical of a lengthy "wash list" of signs and symptoms that could indicate many conditions other than hypoglycemia. Nevertheless, it makes *good sense* to at least rule out hypoglycemia! All persons, especially those with unhealthy lifestyles, who have any of the above listed signs or symptoms, may find that a change to a healthier lifestyle, as described in the following chapters, may well eliminate their problems. To rule out an underlying illness, however, it is obviously essential to obtain medical advice, even if we have only *one* of the above listed signs or symptoms or any other physical or emotional problem. A physical examination and various laboratory tests (including a five-hour Oral Glucose Tolerance Test) may well provide the necessary objective verification of the subjective symptoms.

In my work as a professional counselor and medical psychotherapist, I have seen many dramatic instances where individuals have been set free of what appeared to be intractable problems once hypoglycemia was identified and appropriately treated. In *Victory Over Depression* (1988), I have provided a number of case histories involving individuals diagnosed with low blood sugar, who had such *varied* problems as imprisonment due to asocial behavior, substance abuse, suicidal depression, and recurrent depression. This, however, is only a fraction of the scores of persons I have dealt with over the past twenty-five years with such varied emotional problems as anger, anxiety, depression, fearfulness, insomnia, marital distress, nightmares, addictions, stealing, and temper tantrums, which often proved to have a direct connection to low blood sugar!

Glucose: A Principal Brain Food

When it comes to the brain, it is wise to remember that its principal fuel is glucose, and that any lack of (or other irregularity with) this particular fuel may sometimes have disastrous results. This fuel, transported in our bloodstream as "blood sugar," is vital for every one of our billions of brain cells and trillions of body cells. A few foods can provide an immediate supply of glucose to our blood stream (for example, glucose in some soft drinks) but, in general, our bodies manufacture glucose primarily from carbohydrates, secondarily from protein, and when the former are not available, from fat. Our brain can only burn glucose and goes "haywire" when there is an insufficient supply. A steady and appropriate supply of both glucose and oxygen are utterly essential for proper brain functioning, and, hence, a healthy mental and emotional life. Please note that the oxygen supply to our brain is also impaired with severely low blood sugar. This means double trouble for the brain. Once again, we are reminded that a healthy physical, mental, social, emotional, and even spiritual life is not possible without a balanced diet, which must include complex carbohydrates, protein, and fat.

The Glucose Tolerance Test

The Oral Glucose Tolerance Test (OGTT) has been widely used to determine the role of blood sugar levels in health and disease. Some health professionals, however, refuse to order this test and prefer to rely on other measures. In the meantime, many experts contend that the test *is* important and must be at least five hours in length. They consider less than five hours nondiagnostic and a general waste of time. Following a period of fasting (usually overnight), the blood glucose levels are checked, first before consuming a glucose drink, then at the half-hour level and hourly for up to at least a five-hour period. The test may identify low levels of blood sugar (hypoglycemia), or high levels of blood sugar (diabetes), and may provide information on other conditions, including adrenal and pituitary disorders.

Emotional Problems May Have a Physical Basis

To make a determination of whether a test is normal or not, a physician has to consider many factors, including age, gender, and the physical condition of the person. In general, however, an adult person's glucose tolerance test is considered normal when the fasting blood glucose level is between 80–120 mg/dl, less than 175 mg/dl at the first hour (a rise of approximately 50% is expected by the first hour), less than 140 mg/dl at the second hour, and in the normal range of 80–120 mg/dl at the third and remaining hours.

There are many variables that may increase blood glucose levels, including: arthritis, caffeine, cortisol, diuretics, emotional stress, estrogens, hypertension, infection, liver disease, obesity, oral contraceptives, pregnancy, prolonged inactivity, smoking, and thyroid hormone. Some variables that may *decrease* blood glucose levels include: Addison's disease, alcohol, aspirin, fever, and certain medications. There are also cautions to be observed before administering the OGTT, especially when taking adrenal steroids (cortisone), aspirin in large doses, diuretics, birth-control pills, Dilantin, or L-Dopa, and so forth. A physician may decide to discontinue these substances for several days prior to testing.

Obviously, many factors must be considered by a physician to determine if it is a good idea to administer the OGTT. Contraindications for an oral test may include sprue, celiac disease, hypothyroidism (slow absorption will produce a flat "curve"), thyrotoxicosis (fast absorption will produce a hyperglycemic—diabetic—curve), heart disease (large amounts of glucose may lower serum potassium), and those who had all or part of their stomach removed (Bauer, 1982; Light, 1980, 1981; Brandt, 1988). Under medical supervision, it may indeed be a lot easier, and perhaps wiser, to substitute a change in lifestyle, as outlined in the following chapter, for the OGTT. Even a few weeks on a wellness-oriented diet, for example, could be helpful in overcoming the signs and symptoms of functional hypoglycemia.

Low blood sugar, or major fluctuations in blood sugar levels, are by no means the only physical source for some of our emotional problems. Other sources for emotional problems are sometimes found in allergies, amino acid deficiencies, chemical pollutants in the home or workplace, disease, drugs (toxic reactions are common), mineral deficiencies, problems with neurotransmitters, weather sensitivities, and so forth. I have included a lengthy description of glucose-related issues only because of its all-too-frequently overlooked major role in mental health.

Our Mind Influences Our Brain, and Vice-Versa

It is clear that the body plays a vital role in physical and emotional health, and hence, even spiritual health. There is also overwhelming evidence that our physical well-being is, to a great extent, directly under the control of our mind. It is equally true, however, that our mind is directly influenced by our brain. There are simply no dividers between body, brain, and mind. We are charged to take good care of our bodies, as we are created in God's image, and our bodies are the dwelling place of the Holy Spirit. Any abuse, or willful neglect of our bodies, whether by the consumption of dangerous or harmful products, or through the display of a noncaring attitude, is not pleasing to God. In addition to our responsibility to God, our children, and ourselves, we have a larger social responsibility. Driving our car and finding it difficult to keep our eyes open because of low-blood-sugar-induced narcolepsy is as dangerous as driving a car under the influence of alcohol. If done willfully, it indicates the absence of a social conscience.

10

Some Definite Don'ts for Good Physical Health

> Don't you know that you yourselves are God's temple and that God's Spirit lives in you? If anyone destroys God's temple, God will destroy him; for God's temple is sacred, and you are that temple.
>
> —1 Cor. 3:16–17

God has established specific physical laws and principles for the operation of the universe, and He has also laid out very specific guidelines for His children on earth. Those guidelines include the freedom and responsibility to make good choices. Earlier we looked at the process of choosing from a cognitive point of view and concluded that our feelings and actions are, to a great extent, the final product of our thoughts and beliefs. The Scriptures teach, and history confirms, that our emotions and actions are the outgrowth of our perceptions and cognitions (thoughts, beliefs, and attitudes); "death and life is in the power of the tongue." Even as God permits the demise of local churches when there is discord and dissension, He also permits the demise of those who willfully destroy their own bodies; bodies that are individual and collective temples of God's Holy Spirit.

Our mind is encased within our brain—a complicated network of electrochemical processes. It is of the utmost importance to understand that we cannot think realistically, rationally, or optimistically when our brain is "on the blink," and this often requires that we must help our brain before we can help our mind; a sound mind requires a sound body. Disturbed brain chemistry plays a direct role in poor school performance, delinquency, emotional problems, interpersonal problems, as well as in aggressive and violent behavior. Disturbed brain chemistry (biochemical imbalance) might result from a genetic defect, injury, or illness, but is far more likely the outcome of poor dietary or other negative lifestyle habits. As I have stated throughout this book and elsewhere, it is also possible that disturbed brain chemistry results from disturbed thinking; our mind and our brain continuously influence each other.

In the final analysis, however, it seems that most individuals in our society, most of the time, have an opportunity to choose their destiny, and that includes feelings and behavior. It is unwise, however, to overlook the powerful role that brain chemistry plays in every aspect of human behavior. Poor diet and nutrition are major players in intrapersonal and interpersonal unhappiness, poor intellectual achievement, and even in aggression, delinquency, and violence. Please understand that a malfunctioning body is not necessarily the *cause* of such events as anxiety, depression, delinquency, or violence, but it is very often a primary *source*. If our brain doesn't function right, our mind doesn't function right either, and our thinking, feelings, and actions will be directly influenced by this. It's a simple, yet constantly overlooked, equation.

This chapter, and the next, can only touch on a few important aspects of good physical health. It is by no means an exhaustive treatise. In order to more fully comprehend the importance of a healthy lifestyle, it is wise to buy a number of good books on this subject, subscribe to a few pertinent magazines, and/or to seek assistance from local libraries, the Internet, or other sources. In order to accept responsibility for our health, we must stay up-to-date on new and useful information that constantly comes to light. But remember, it remains necessary to seek medical advice before making changes in diet or physical lifestyle. With these reminders and precautions in mind, let's have a brief look at some often recommended don'ts for good physical health.

Here Are Some Don'ts

Don't Use Tobacco Products

The use of any tobacco product, in any form, is one of the most self-destructive health practices a person could possibly have. Millions of persons have died because of tobacco! Those who know about the incredible dangers of smoking, and yet continue with this admittedly difficult, but not-impossible-to-break habit or addiction, are committing a form of unintentional suicide, and perhaps even unintentional homicide. Smokers risk reducing their own life-span, while at the same time, they risk reducing the life-span of their loved ones. They need to give some thought to the part they might well play in the horrible deaths of thousands of persons annually in the United States, who are said to be victims of secondhand smoke. And what about exposing those who have allergies and lung diseases to tobacco smoke?

It seems incomprehensible that in an enlightened or civilized country, anyone would want to put cancer-causing and addictive substances in their bodies, but in the United States, we find that over 25% of the adult population (about fifty million individuals) continues to smoke in spite of numerous warnings of its health hazards and the wide availability of smoking-cessation programs.

One reason why some individuals may have been unable to overcome their smoking addiction, may be found in a coexisting alcohol dependence. Since alcohol dependence often goes hand-in-hand with hypoglycemia, it might also be more difficult to stop smoking without also stopping the use of alcohol, caffeine, refined sugar, and their related products.

Those who want to quit smoking must set a firm date to do so. They should seek a medical evaluation, family or other support systems, and trust in God to set them free from this physical and psychological enslavement. As the leading cause of preventable death in this country, it is imperative that we break the bondage of tobacco and assist those who are in the clutches of this ruthless killer. Please note that the abrupt cessation of smoking may lead to various signs and symptoms of *nicotine withdrawal*, including depression, sleeplessness, irritability, anger, anxiety, and restlessness. Medical supervision is important for all individuals who want to stop smoking, but this is especially true for those who take medications. Smoking cessation may alter the rate at which some medications are absorbed by the body.

Don't Use Alcohol

Alcohol is a poison that slowly and insidiously deteriorates our health, as it effects our nervous, endocrine, and immune systems. About ten million individuals in this country are seriously addicted to alcohol. The use of alcohol and tobacco are the two most powerful health-devastating habits in our society. Its costs are also enormous—a cost borne by all of society.

Is alcoholism a disease? Leading experts disagree with one another on this issue. An eminent American scholar, Professor Herbert Fingarette of the University of California, cited two hundred forty-three publications, covering the period of 1952–1986 and concluded that the popular belief that alcoholism is a disease is only a myth (Fingarette, 1988). Disease or no disease, we *know* that if we don't drink alcohol, we don't become addicted. We also know that continued use of alcohol leads to both physical and/or psychological dependence, and that the combination of alcohol with antihistamines, barbiturates, tranquilizers, and many other drugs is extremely dangerous.

We know that alcohol is a brain depressant and that it leads to serious illness and untimely death. We also know that alcohol is a carcinogen (cancer causing substance), linked to cancer of the esophagus, larynx, mouth, and liver. There are many alcohol-re-

Some Definite Don'ts for Good Physical Health

lated disorders, including: *alcohol-induced intoxication, delirium* (an acute mental disorder with confusion, hallucinations, illusions, and irrational/violent behavior), *dementia* (impaired intellectual functioning), *persisting amnestic disorder* (a long-term, persistent memory disturbance), *psychotic disorder, mood disorder, anxiety disorder, sleep disorder,* and *sexual dysfunction.* No one who is truly aware of the indescribable grief and harm caused by alcohol can rationally defend its production, distribution, sale, or use.

The problem with alcohol, however, is likely going to get worse before it gets better unless the government, the organized church, and every one with a social conscience, finally becomes tired of the destruction of our citizens on the road, damage to innocent individuals (especially children), burdens on the criminal justice system, and a lengthy list of other major social issues. In spite of all the destruction that can so readily be observed, there are still those who come to the defense of alcohol. Of course, someone might say, it is not the alcohol that kills, but the reckless use of alcohol. This brings us to a common myth.

A myth held by many, and readily used by special interest groups, claims that there is a safe amount of alcohol that can be consumed. Consider the work of Axel Gustafson (1884), who believed that a safe dietary dose of alcohol existed. After researching scholarly works on the subject of alcohol at the British Museum in London, he came to the opposite conclusion. The extent of Gustafson's research was of enormous proportions. He consulted three thousand scholarly works from various countries that had been published between 1483 and 1883—a period of four hundred years. Here are just a few of the three thousand scholarly works studied by Gustafson:

> Michael Schrick, *Von dem geprannten wassern in welcher mass man die zu den gelydern prauchen soll,* Germany, 1483; Philip Stubes, *The Anatomies of Abuse,* 1583, Great Britain; C. Lipinski, *De actionum potionum spiritisorum in corpus humanum,* Russia, 1821; E. Labarthe, *De l'influence de alcohol dans la production de maladies,* France, 1829; Lehmann, *Ueber die Folgen des*

Missbrauchs der Geistigen Getranke, Switzerland, 1837; Moses Rosenthal, *De la misere des classes laborieuses en Angletere et en France,* Belgium, 1858; Antonio Tagliabue, *Il Suicido,* Italy, 1871; J. Moreno, E. *Apustes sobre el empleo therepeutico del Alcohol,* Mexico, 1871; Florent Van der Ven, *Het misbruik van sterke dranken,* Holland, 1873; J. H. Kellogg, *The physical, moral, and social effects of alcoholic poison as a beverage and as a medicine,* Battle Creek, Michigan, USA, 1876.

As I read the original 1884 edition of Gustafson's book, I wondered how many of today's eager advocates for the moderate use of alcohol have taken the time to thoroughly study this subject in depth? While alcohol's death roll keeps growing longer day after day, we have the same old arguments that have been observed for centuries. There is indeed nothing new under the sun!

Even *if* alcohol in small quantities would not be detrimental to a person's health, and even *if* it might have some beneficial effects, we would still have to find a human brain that is not easily addicted. Such a brain, to my knowledge, does not exist. We know that most individuals cannot even handle the addictive nature of sugar or prevent its bad effects on their physical and emotional health. Can we then, in good conscience, recommend the so-called moderate use of alcohol? (See also Gen. 9:20–27; 19:31–38; Prov. 20:1; 23:29–35; Isa. 5:11–12; Hab. 2:5; Rom. 14:21; Eph. 5:18.)

Don't Use Caffeine

After looking at the incredibly destructive nature of tobacco and alcohol, it may seem that caffeine is somewhat of a nonproblem. Hundreds of millions of individuals are using caffeine products on a daily basis and *seemingly* do so without much of a problem. Just because we don't readily observe a problem does not mean there is no problem.

Many of the happy faces leaving some coffee bar early in the morning, will, later in the day, turn into the unhappy faces of cranky and argumentative individuals with caffeine edginess. For

Some Definite Don'ts for Good Physical Health

many individuals, caffeine is at first only a mild mood elevator, minor stimulant, or pleasant diversion. All too often, however, caffeine becomes a source of problems. Caffeine, like alcohol and nicotine, *is* an addictive drug. It is not the innocent substance that so many believe it to be. It is an alkaloid, found not only in coffee, but also in tea, cola drinks, chocolate, diet aids, and other products. It is, of course, a "marvelous" product for those who market it. After all, caffeine is a substance that creates habitual users. Like those who are hooked on alcohol or nicotine, they will always be back for more.

Many individuals who might snub their noses at "druggies," can barely open their own eyes in the morning unless they first have their caffeine fix. This early morning ritual might need to be repeated regularly throughout the day with more coffee, soft drinks, or other caffeine-containing products. In addition to its addictive nature, caffeine has a negative effect on the central nervous system (spinal cord and brain), and many individuals come to suffer with so-called "caffeinism," which reveals itself in anxiety, excitement, insomnia, irregular heartbeats, nervousness, and other symptoms. Caffeine is of special concern to those who have hypoglycemia. These individuals should not touch caffeine in any amount, in any form, at any time.

There are those, I am sure, who may think it is ridiculous to take such a hard line against caffeine. Those, however, who have seen the fallout from this seemingly innocent product, don't think so at all. Many individuals are very vulnerable to caffeine because their nervous and endocrine systems are already stressed to the max, or because they have high blood pressure, irregular heartbeats, low blood sugar, high cholesterol, fibrocystic disease, or other health problems. Now add to all of this the problem of coffee itself, quite apart from caffeine. Many warnings have been issued over the years that coffee is bad for our health and may be implicated in cancer of the bladder and pancreas. It seems that many individuals are undergoing unnecessary suffering because of problems with both coffee and/or caffeine.

I will give just one example: A young woman was referred to me because of her anxiety attacks. Tense and extremely worried, she told me that she had recently experienced some life-threatening episodes. One evening, while attending a lecture, her heart started to race and would not stop doing so. Taken to the nearest emergency room, a physician decided that she should be hospitalized. With medication and rest, her heart rate came down, and after a day, she was released from the hospital. Shortly thereafter, however, the same thing happened. Once again the young woman was hospitalized. The doctors decided to do a number of additional tests. All of these tests were negative, and the doctors concluded that this young woman was suffering from anxiety and needed psychological help.

During her first visit to my office, I traced every step she took on the day in question—whatever she was thinking, feeling, or doing from the moment she got up, till the moment the attack took place. She recalled that she had gone to an out-of-town lecture. On the way to the lecture, she stopped to buy a soft drink. She was hungry and thirsty and believed that a cola beverage might take care of her problem. She drank the beverage en route to the meeting place, where shortly after arrival, she had her frightening experience. Some time after the experience, she had a similar episode, but this time at home.

This is what I found: The independent variable that caused her first attack was a cola drink, and the independent variable that caused her second attack was one cup of black coffee. The one thing that these two beverages had in common was caffeine, and the effect in either case was identical—a severe attack of tachycardia. Only a few common-sense dietary changes were necessary to change this young woman's life around. She did not have an anxiety disorder but a common physical vulnerability (see chapter 9). A rare case? Hardly.

There are many individuals who are at risk with caffeine. Since caffeine temporarily increases blood pressure, it is very unwise to use caffeine if we have hypertension or are experiencing excessive stress. Caffeine is also contraindicated for those who use birth control pills, appetite suppressors, tranquilizers (such as Valium or Xanax), or so-called MAOs (Monoamine Oxidase Inhibitors) for depression. Caffeine is found in many products, but we must be especially alert to the high amounts of caffeine in brewed coffee, caffeinated cola drinks, and some over-the-counter drugs used for colds, headaches, and so forth. It is important to read labels and to ask physicians and pharmacists about possible drug/caffeine interactions. Relatively low dosages of caffeine are found in chocolate bars or cocoa drinks, but here we find high dosages of another problematic substance: sucrose!

Only five of the following symptoms need to be present to indicate the possibility of caffeine intoxication: restlessness, nervousness, excitement, insomnia, flushed face, diuresis, gastrointestinal disturbances, muscle twitching, rambling flow of thought and speech, tachycardia or arrhythmia, periods of inexhaustibility, and psychomotor agitation (DSM-IV, APA 1994). Caffeine intoxication may result from as few as two to three cups of brewed coffee (and sometimes even less than that). Other disorders that may result from the use of caffeine include Caffeine-Induced Anxiety Disorder, and Caffeine-Induced Sleep Disorder. Caffeine, in spite of its great popularity, is a true health hazard. Those who think differently are kidding themselves or perhaps don't care.

Questions that are frequently raised, include: "Why can't we have just one or two cups of coffee, one or two drinks of alcohol, or one or two cigarettes? . . . Isn't moderation the key? . . . Why do we have to be such fanatics?" There are several reasons, but the biggest reason why we cannot use a little bit of an addictive substance such as alcohol, caffeine, or nicotine, is that sooner or later we may get hooked. That is also why it is nonproductive to teach people to simply cut back on addictive substances. This can only be done if there is a well-established goal to eventually quit. When it comes to addictive substances, we must take a firm stand: quit!

Don't Use Sugar

If the previous sections seemed rather harsh, then things may go from bad to worse in this section. I do not have any axes to grind, however, and I am well aware that "there is no condemnation for those who are in Christ Jesus" (Rom. 8:1). But, if our objective is to have a renewed mind and transformed life, we need to realize that all too many individuals do not even get close to this goal because they make the mistake of seeing themselves in some kind of spiritual "bubble"—automatically protected from negative physical factors. They perhaps fail to see that we are spiritual, as well as physical, and emotional beings. We dare not neglect any one of these three parts. On earth our mind exists as an intregal part of our brain. If we neglect our body or brain, we are likely also to neglect our mind, and, hence, our spiritual life. And what does all of this have to do with sugar? It has a lot to do with it! Disturbed brains create disturbed minds. Let's see how sugar may play a part in this.

First, a little additional background. For about twenty-five years, I have had ample opportunity to observe in day-to-day practice the cause and effect of sugar on the emotional and physical health of many individuals I have counseled. And I am not alone. Distinguished physicians and researchers, such as Professor John Yudkin of London University (Yudkin, 1972), and Surgeon-Captain T. L. Cleave of the Royal British Navy and Director of Medical Research at the Institute of Naval Medicine (Cleave, 1974), as well as dozens of other scientists and observers, long ago concluded that sugar is bad for our health. Both Yudkin and Cleave, for example, were very adamant that sugar is dangerous for the simple reason that it is a killer, as in the case of diabetes. Many studies have been done on the connection between sugar and illness. Sugar feeds bacteria, another growing problem today, and also feeds yeast, as in health-debilitating candidiasis. Another researcher, E. M. Abrahamson (1977), with a doctorate in chemistry as well as medicine, found that physical, mental, and emotional health was often adversely affected by hypoglycemia, or as he called it, "sugar starvation."

Powerful interest groups, and many others, continue to believe and publicize that sugar is not only harmless, but may actually be good for us as part of a "healthy diet." Sugar addiction is one of the

Some Definite Don'ts for Good Physical Health

primary reasons, if not *the* primary reason behind obesity. Several studies have found that the excessive consumption of refined sugar upsets the chemical balance of body and brain. It raises cortisol, cholesterol, and triglyceride levels. Refined sugar, more so than fat, is a primary source of excessive weight and obesity (Brandt, 1978). High-sucrose loads have also been found to contribute to strokes, migraines, hypertension, bowel disease, dental caries, and other conditions. Aggressive behavior has also repeatedly been linked to the excessive use of refined sugars. Several studies noted that it was possible to reduce disciplinary actions by significantly lowering the sugar intake of juvenile offenders (Rodale, 1968). When it comes to aggressive behavior, juvenile delinquency, or violence, it will be found that hypoglycemia is, at times, a factor. Those who are prone to asocial behaviors might more readily do so with low blood glucose levels or major glucose fluctuations (Schauss, 1981).

It's not possible to adequately describe the many health dangers that are inherent in the use of refined sugar in the few limited paragraphs of this chapter. There are, however, dozens of good books on this subject that can be found in bookstores and libraries. Those who dig long and hard will discover, among other things, that refined sugar is a fuel for cancer cells and other disease processes, that it suppresses the appetite for healthier foods, and weakens the immune system. While some individuals are seemingly not affected by the modern "sugar plague," many others pay dearly for their love affair with a "sweet seducer." We must be careful with reports that sugar is not harmful. Some of that advice comes from well-meaning individuals, as well as from those who have deeply vested interests. Once again, the proof of the pudding may be found in *not* eating it. If the elimination of refined carbohydrates (such as white bread, white rice, spaghetti, cakes, cookies, candy, ice-cream, and especially sugars, such as sucrose and glucose) make us healthier and happier, then what are we waiting for?

Don't Use or Do Anything That Impairs Health

It would be very difficult, and extremely boring, to live by an endless list of things to avoid for good health. In this short section, however, we need to take a brief look at the larger picture. Threats to good physical health are found not only in the use of addictive substances such as alcohol, caffeine, sugar, and tobacco, but also in the use of such illegal substances as cannabis, cocaine, hallucinogens, inhalants, opioids, and similar junk. We also need a greater awareness of the many environmental sources that interfere with our health and, ultimately, our life!

We must do all we can to prevent the destruction of our health. This includes staying away from such health hazards as junk food, addictive substances, a sedentary lifestyle, unnecessary medications, illegal substances, environmental pollutants (such as neurotoxic agents and carcinogens), excessive stress, violent "sports," reckless driving, and work addiction. We need a greater appreciation and reverence for life—we need to come to our senses. We need to do this now!

11

Some Important Do's for Good Physical Health

"May God himself, the God of peace, sanctify you through and through. May your whole spirit, soul and body be kept blameless at the coming of our Lord Jesus Christ."
—1 Thess. 5:23

God wants us to be sanctified, but we already know that this is an impossible task on our own. We are in need of constant guidance; ultimately, only God can sanctify us. Yet we are players, called to do our part. We are to reject all harm to our bodies or anything that hinders attaining a transformed and victorious life. Because of a direct link between them, and other reasons as well, we must take good care of our spiritual, emotional, and physical life. In this chapter, we consider a few important steps to insure that our bodies are as healthy as possible.

Here Are Some Do's for Good Physical Health

MAINTAIN WEIGHT CONTROL

One very important step for good physical health is to have some control over our weight. Actually, God warns us to be careful with food and drink. Listen to this warning from the book of Proverbs: "Do not join those who drink too much wine or gorge themselves on meat, for drunkards and gluttons become poor, and drowsiness clothes them in rags." (Prov. 23:20; also see Deut. 21:20). Contrary to a widely-held myth, it is possible for the vast majority of overweight persons to lose a good deal of excess weight. While this is not always an easy thing to do, it is unwise to search for excuses, rather than solutions.

Being overweight is nearly always the final result of *excessive caloric intake* (eating too much); *insufficient caloric output* (being too immobile); *consuming unhealthy foods* (eating junk food); *and clinging to self-defeating beliefs* (lying to ourselves), with statements such as: "When I start eating I cannot stop," "I have no will power," "It is not fair to deprive myself," "I am too overweight to exercise," or "I cannot resist certain foods." This combination of an irrational lifestyle and irrational thinking is at the root of the problem for most overweight individuals.

The above insight holds true, even in those cases where an excessive caloric intake is in response to specific physiological, environmental, socioeconomic, psychological, or other stimuli. Overeating is often a response, for example, to an allergy, low blood sugar, depression, sexual abuse, or people pushing food on non-assertive individuals. In addition, there are many theories as to why people are overweight, including the *cell theory* (adipose cells are fixed in early years), *metabolic theory* (endocrine dysfunction), and *glucostatic theory* (dysfunction of the appetite regulating mechanism in the hypothalamus). These theories are interesting and worthwhile but are all too often used as an excuse by those who simply eat too much food, eat the wrong foods, and/or fail to burn up sufficient calories with work or exercise. My experience over the past twenty-five years has shown that conscientiously following the guidelines of this chapter under the supervision of a physician, can lead to acceptable weight control for many, if not most individuals (Brandt, 1978).

GET REGULAR EXERCISE

The benefits of regular exercise are so fantastic and have been so well-publicized that it is a mystery why so many individuals still don't realize that exercise is a key factor in both the prevention and cure of disease. Regular exercise is of the greatest importance for good health, high energy levels, greater productivity, increased longevity, and stress reduction. Because regular and vigorous exercise changes the chemical composition of our bodies for the better, we can deal more effectively with the challenges of daily life. Not only does exercise improve the quality of life, it also extends it. Exercise can reduce the biological age of a middle-aged person by as many as ten, or even twenty years. There is simply no question at all that exercise can help us to be healthier and happier. God created our bodies in such as way that they need regular exercise. If we fail to do this, we age prematurely, lose resistance to a variety of diseases, become more prone to emotional difficulties, and have less energy. Before starting on an exercise program, however, it is essential to get a thorough physical evaluation. This is all the more important for elderly, out of shape individuals, or anyone who has health concerns. It is also important to fully investigate the type of exercise that is best suited for a particular person.

The many benefits that can be obtained from moderate or vigorous regular exercise include: slowing the aging process, preventing heart problems, reducing fatty substances such as cholesterol and triglycerides, strengthening the heart muscle, providing the brain with increased oxygen supply and other nutrients, improving metabolism, providing sounder sleep, and many other wonderful benefits. For maximum effectiveness, exercise must remain fun. It must not be overly competitive, hurried, stressful, or demanding. Walking, cycling, and swimming are among the best exercises. These exercises are also inexpensive and can be done alone or with others. Whenever exercise brings on pain, dizziness,

The Renewed Mind

nausea, or other physical problems, it is time to immediately stop and obtain new medical advice. As stated earlier, we must never start an exercise program without first obtaining a thorough medical examination.

Get Sufficient Sleep

It is not possible to stay healthy for long, or to recover from illness, without sufficient rest and sleep. Sufficient sleep is essential for a healthy, happy, and successful life. The majority of adults need at least eight hours of sleep daily for good health and longevity. Whenever we are sleep deprived, we are unable to function at our best. It is believed that, in this country, as many as one in two adults are sleep-deprived. There are many reasons for sleep deprivation in our modern society, including: shift work, extensive travel, late television-watching, poor dietary practices that lead to wakefulness at night, lack of physical exercise, sleep disorders, and emotional problems. The quality of our life depends just as much on sound sleep as it does on good nutrition and regular exercise.

The Scriptures remind us that "sound judgment and discernment" are important if we wish to "lie down in sweet sleep" (Prov. 3: 21–24). God wants us to sleep in peace, so that we may refresh ourselves and be able to function at optimum levels. During sleep, our muscles relax; heart rate, blood pressure, body temperature, and cortisol output are reduced; and there is a mental exclusion of external stressors. These are all stress reductive measures—body, brain, and mind, all get some rest. These sleep activities are the opposite of what takes place during periods of stress, where we find an increase in muscle tension, heart rate, blood pressure, body temperature, cortisone output, and an inclusion of external stressors. Sleep is a wonderful stress antidote!

To help us sleep better we need to:

- Eliminate sleep-pattern disrupters, such as alcohol, caffeine, nicotine, and sleep medications, as well as carbohydrate snacks shortly before bedtime.
- Only do light exercises or light work in the evening hours.

Some Important Do's for Good Physical Health

- Take a short walk before going to bed or listen to some soothing music.
- Do not go to bed hungry. Perhaps eat a high-protein *and* complex carbohydrate snack (e.g. a small turkey sandwich made with whole grain bread) and/or drink a small glass of warm milk.
- Establish a regular bedtime routine. Stick to a wake-up and bedtime schedule. This must include at least an eight hour sleep/rest period. If necessary, use an alarm clock as a reminder to go to bed.
- Set a comfortable temperature for the bedroom. When the bedroom is either too hot or too cold, it may affect dream patterns negatively.
- Do not force sleep. It is better to read some light literature or listen to relaxing music until we are ready to fall asleep, or fall asleep again.
- Drink a cup of soothing tea shortly before bedtime—for example chamomile, passion flower, or lemon balm.
- Do not watch disturbing television programs, or read upsetting materials in the evenings, if at all!
- Meditate on one of the Psalms—for example, the twenty-third Psalm.

FOLLOW A "WELLNESS" DIET

What we eat and drink is either good or bad for us. There is no neutral zone when it comes to diet. Most health-oriented diets stress that *refined* carbohydrates (especially sugar) have no place at all in the diet of those who suffer with *artheriosclerosis, atherosclerosis, cancer, candidiasis, cardiovascular disease, cirrhosis of the liver, Crohn's disease, depression, diabetes* (except to balance an insulin reaction), *diverticulitis, endometriosis, fungal infections, gallbladder disorders, gout, herpes, hypoglycemia, hypothyroidism, indigestion,* and scores of other disorders. Diet, next to such destructive habits such as using alcohol and tobacco, is to blame for most of our ill health. Many experts, over the past fifty years, have urged the avoidance of processed and refined foods and have stressed that we need to eat more living foods, especially raw vegetables and fruits. Likewise, they have warned us to greatly limit our intake of (or exclude) meat, table salt, alcohol, caffeine, and sugar.

Even the United States Government has, on several occasions, informed the American public about their unhealthy dietary practices, but these attempts have been rather lukewarm and fiercely opposed by all special interest groups. The diet and lifestyle recommendations provided by independent medical researchers and practitioners, such as Dr. Alex Forbes (*The Bristol Diet*), Dr. James F. Balch and Phyllis Balch (*Prescription for Nutritional Healing*), Dr. Robert A. Anderson (*Wellness Medicine*), and many others, deserve our full and undivided attention. Health conscious individuals need to start their own wellness-lifestyle library to become better informed on the many things they can do to have a happier, healthier, and more productive life. And although I disagree with her views on the moderate use of wine, one of the first books to include in that library would be *Does The Bible Teach Nutrition?* by Elizabeth Baker (Winepress Publishing, 1997). As stated before, it is not possible to have an optimally healthy mind if our brain is deficient in certain nutrients. An undernourished or malnourished brain may result in a poorly functioning mind and make it difficult to lead a constructive and happy life.

How well we think is directly linked to how well we live. Mental, emotional, or personality issues are not only matters of a spiritual or educational nature. These issues cannot be separated from a well-functioning brain and body. Nutritional deficiencies, for example, may greatly interfere with our ability to think rationally and make wise decisions. The following nutritional guidelines consist of suggestions we may wish to consider and discuss with our healthcare providers. Always seek professional advice.

Some Basic Nutritional Guidelines

For several decades, we have had a virtually uninterrupted flow of new nutritional information. As a rule, most of this has been very helpful, and occasionally, even lifesaving. On the other hand, there has also been plenty of conflicting and confusing information. The field of dietetics and nutrition is not as scientific as we might like to believe. Nevertheless, it seems that there are some universally-accepted and useful findings that we may want to investigate and perhaps incorporate into our wellness-oriented nutritional program.

Here are some nutritional products that are often recommended in wellness-oriented diets:

- Beverages—Distilled, spring, or purified water; certain herbal teas, for example, chamomile and passion flower; decaffeinated green tea; soy milk; and fresh, homemade fruit juices.
- Dairy—Butter; white cheeses; unsweetened low-fat yogurt; low-fat and skimmed milk. Except for skimmed milk, it is generally believed that dairy products are to be consumed in small quantities only, if at all.
- Eggs—Hailed or despised by different "experts," it seems that a moderate approach is probably in order. Egg white is an excellent source of protein, and an egg yolk has many vitamins, for example: A, B1, B2, B3 (niacin), B5, B6, B12, D, E, F, H (biotin), M (folic acid), and choline. Those who have high blood cholesterol levels might be advised differently, but most other individuals might well be allowed an egg every other day, as part of an overall wellness diet.
- Food supplements—Food supplements are highly concentrated elements of food products believed to be beneficial in both the prevention and treatment of various physical and emotional problems. Many health experts believe that to rely solely on food products may not be sufficient for maintaining or restoring health. They believe that the use of specific food supplements, or a multivitamin/mineral supplement, is often necessary. In this highly competitive and lucrative field, it is important to obtain sound professional advice from one or more financially disinterested sources.
- Fish—Preferably broiled, or baked, fresh white fish; but also salmon, sardines, and herring, for their beneficial fish

The Renewed Mind

oils. Some experts recommend that we don't use more than six total ounces per day of fish, poultry, *or* meat.
- Fruit—Virtually all wellness diets stress the importance of eating a lot of fruit everyday.
- Grains and seeds—Here it is important to look for plenty of fiber and to use a variety of grains and brans. Unless allergic to certain grain products (for example, wheat), most individuals are usually advised to have several helpings every day of rye, oats, whole wheat, buckwheat, millet, brown rice, spelt, and so forth. Whole seeds, especially flax, sunflower, and pumpkin seeds, are also important.
- Meat Products—The controversy among "experts" over eating meat products is still unresolved, but it seems clear that many individuals are feeling far healthier on a vegetarian diet. I personally believe the latter is best. In any case, it is wise to eat only very small quantities of meat, (preferably *lean* beef), poultry (preferably chicken or turkey), or a recommended fish selection.
- Nuts—Fresh nuts are highly recommended, but, because of their high caloric content, only in small quantities.
- Oils—The most consistently recommended oils are canola and olive oils.
- Seasoning and spices—Chives, garlic, ginger, onions, nutmeg, marjoram, and other seasonings. Light salt, a mixture of potassium and sodium, is usually allowed in moderation.
- Soups—Homemade soups prepared from healthy whole food products as listed in this section.
- Sprouts—All sprouts are recommended—for example, alfalfa, lentils, and peas.
- Sweets—Only those sweets made with natural fruit or fruit juices, or small quantities of honey, are normally recommended in wellness-oriented diets.
- Vegetables—Here we find one of the keys to good health. Large quantities of fresh (or if necessary, frozen) vegetables, especially in the raw state, are highly recommended. Especially included are dark green, leafy vegetables such as spin-

ach, endive, and so forth. Other excellent vegetables are broccoli, cabbage, and carrots.

Having considered some of the usually recommended food products, we may also want to take a quick look at the usually *nonrecommended* food products. These include virtually all artificial, carbonated, colored, fried, imitation, processed, refined, roasted, salted, or sweetened products. Specifically excluded from every wellness diet are alcohol, caffeine, canned or bottled soft drinks, fatty foods, hydrogenated fats, shortening, processed cereals, refined sugars of any kind, and other refined products such as white flour, white rice, cookies, donuts or pies. The number of commonly-used products that are considered unhealthy is quite lengthy and is beyond the scope of this book.

There are many opinions as to what constitutes a wellness (health-oriented) diet. As a general guideline, however, we can say that most individuals need a varied diet that is rich in fresh fruits, vegetables, nuts, seeds, and whole grains; supplemented with fish, poultry, lean beef, low-fat dairy products, and eggs. If properly selected, such a diet would consist mainly of raw foods, and would provide, among other things, the amino acids, enzymes, phytochemicals, fatty acids, vitamins, and minerals needed by our body.

There is no universal agreement on the exact percentages of fat, protein, or complex carbohydrates that are to be included in a wellness diet. Because there are constantly new reports in this regard, it is wise to consult as many current and reliable sources as possible. The information provided in this section, however, is generally in agreement with US government dietary guidelines and modern health organizations that are concerned with the destructive dietary habits of our nation. There is, thankfully, a rapidly growing interest in the use of specific foods and food supplements in both the prevention and treatment of many physical, as well as emotional, problems. Contrary to many myths that abound, this is a very necessary, timely, and research-driven movement.

Stay Informed on Health Issues

Numerous scientific papers and research reports are available to backup claims that there are nutritional answers for many of our health problems, including so-called degenerative diseases. Unhappily, many well-meaning conservative professionals are decades behind in this regard. This is partly due to allopathic medicine, which uses mainly chemical compounds that are antagonistic or incompatible to the diseases they seek to treat.

This approach, while often helpful and even lifesaving, has failed to put a solid dent into a growing problem with so-called degenerative diseases and is now facing a worldwide crisis in the treatment of many infectious diseases that have become resistant to antibiotics. And whatever success is achieved, comes at a steep price in both money and lives. It is believed, for example, that more than one-hundred thousand persons die annually in this country from prescription drugs alone. Because of the real dangers inherent in the use of many modern medications, we find that neither physicians, pharmacists, nor pharmaceutical companies will assume much responsibility for them. All patients now receive a pamphlet or leaflet that warns of the dangers that are inherent in their prescribed medications. We have a real dilemma on our hands, and it is very important to recognize that our first line of defense in the prevention and treatment of many illnesses is, undoubtedly, a healthy lifestyle, and in particular, a healthy diet and regular exercise. I have included a few words on the status of modern medicine, not to alarm or to deride anyone, but to make it clear that we must be participators, and not mere spectators, when it comes to matters of health, happiness, and success in life.

Because each person's health situation is uniquely different, and because it takes special training to address specific health issues, it is very important not to make health-related decisions, such as dietary changes, without seeking competent medical advice. It is also important to know there is no "universal diet" that is good for everyone. Some healthy foods, or normally useful food supplements, may be harmful for specific individuals, including those who are taking certain medications, have specific medical conditions, are pregnant, and so forth. Individuals who are using food supplements (even if prescribed by a health practitioner) do well to purchase a few helpful books on this subject, such as *Prescription for Nutritional Healing* (Balch and Balch, 1997), *Encyclopedia of Natural Medicine* (Murray and Pizzorno, 1991), *Wellness Medicine* (Anderson, 1987), *Does the Bible Teach Nutrition?* (Baker, 1997), and the *PDR for Herbal Medicines* (PDR, 1999).

Last, but not least, we must not become obsessed with health or beauty. Especially the latter can easily become idolatry. Christian believers also recognize that the absence of physical health is not necessarily one's fault, some kind of divine punishment, or a demonstrated lack of faith. We live in a world governed by natural and spiritual laws. Heredity, childhood experiences, accidents, and so forth, are just a few of the many elements over which we may have no control. God's mercy and grace are far more important than inappropriate condemnation by others, or ourselves!

Always Look to God

Speaking of condemnation, we must be very careful that we do not place others under condemnation because of what they eat or don't eat. The Scriptures do clearly prohibit this (1 Tim. 4:3–5). The Bible does provide us, however, with some helpful guidelines for a healthy lifestyle. We are reminded, for example, to be good stewards, use our talents, and stay away from foolishness. We are further reminded that we are created in God's image and that our body is the temple of the Holy Spirit, which we are to present as a "living sacrifice," and in which, "Christ will be exalted. . . ." (Gen. 1:26,27; 1 Cor. 6:19; Rom. 12:1; Phil. 1:20).

God created excellent food sources for us on this planet by which we could optimally sustain our life—if we wanted to do so. This is what we read in Genesis 1:29: ". . . I give you every seed-bearing plant on the face of the whole earth and every tree that has fruit with seed in it. They will be yours for food." The diet that God originally intended for us to have was clearly a vegetarian diet. This fact did not change until after the flood had destroyed the earth's vegetation. It was only at that time that God granted permission to eat flesh foods: "Everything that lives and moves will be food for you. Just as I gave you the green plants, I now give you everything" (Gen. 9:3).

Another reason why God allowed flesh foods was in response to the complaints of the children of Israel: ". . . I have heard the grumbling of the Israelites. Tell them, 'At twilight you will eat meat, and in the morning you will be filled with bread. Then you will know that I am the LORD your God'" (Exod. 16:12, 13). It remained forbidden, however, to eat blood and fat as described in Lev. 3:17; 7:23, 25. We can clearly see the continued application of God's wisdom in our lives.

The Bible, of course, is as up-to-date as ever, for we are increasingly aware that we must be careful with animal fat, which has been repeatedly associated with higher mortality rates and shortened life spans. High-fat diets and high-sugar diets may lead to premature aging. Green vegetables and fruit, on the other hand, are among the healthiest foods on earth and may lead to increased longevity. The Bible, that marvelously and divinely inspired Word of God, is truly "a lamp for our feet,"—a wonderful book of faith and reason!

Part Five:

The Renewed Mind

12

Some Aspects of Unhealthy Personality Styles

> Brothers, stop thinking like children. In regards to evil be infants, but in your thinking be adults.
> —1 Cor. 14:20

As adults, we must not only "stop thinking like children," but we must also stop clinging to unhealthy personality styles that may prevent us from having happy and healthy relationships. Over the years, I have come to believe that some Christians never come close to having a Christian personality (renewed mind), because they failed to recognize that salvation does not necessarily include a complete personality overhaul. There are many wonderful persons who have been "saved by grace through faith," who desire to have a renewed mind and transformed life, but who still retain one or more unhealthy personality styles or personality disorders.

Unhealthy personality styles are found in those individuals—believers and unbelievers alike—who have a number of specific personality traits that consistently create difficulties for themselves or others. Some of these traits have genetic connections, but more likely, they are the result of early-life experiences. Regrettably, unhealthy personality styles are often a source of many difficulties, including: dysfunctional emotions, marital distress, poor health, and spiritual difficulties.

As long as we are driven by antisocial, dependent, compulsive, narcissistic, or other unhealthy personality styles, it will be difficult, if not impossible, to attain a renewed mind. Some may think that as long as we repent of our sins and accept Christ, that our old unhealthy personalities are completely gone. "After all," they might say, "we are 'new creatures in Christ.'" The latter is true; we are new creatures in Christ, but only in a spiritual sense. We are newly-created spiritual beings; we have been born again. God, at first, created us out of the dust of the earth; He gave us physical life. Now, through Christ, He also changes our spiritual status and moves us from spiritual darkness to light. God gives us a new spiritual life!

Once separated from God, we are now reconciled to Him (cf. 2 Col. 11:21) and given a wonderful opportunity to be His "fellow-workers" (1 Cor. 3:9). Now we can become more Christ-like, start the task of removing mental or emotional strongholds from our minds, and begin to "work out our own salvation in fear and trembling" (Phil. 2:12). We can do this by removing sinful behaviors, negative conditioning, and all other hindrances, including unhealthy personality styles that stand in the way of having a renewed mind and transformed life.

It is with the above thoughts in mind that we are to read the following pages, which describe unhealthy personality styles. It is also important to understand that this chapter is merely informative in nature. It describes various unhealthy personality styles, and only once in a while offers a little hint as to what we can do about them. The latter is best left to the next chapters, which describe a healthy personality, the secret of a Christian person's happiness, and the importance of having not only a healthy personality, but a Christian personality—a renewed mind.

Some Aspects of Unhealthy Personality Styles

What Is an Unhealthy Personality Style?

The majority of individuals in our society can readily identify with one or more of the unhealthy personality styles described in this chapter, but a word of caution is in order. Most of us have only a disposition toward one or more of these personality styles. As fallible and imperfect human beings, all of us have some scattered self-defeating personality traits.

Before we read this chapter, we need to understand what makes a personality style unhealthy. "Unhealthy personality styles," I said elsewhere (Brandt,1998), "are found in those individuals who have several distinct and enduring traits which *consistently* result in difficulties for themselves or others. There are, however, countless individuals, including those with healthy personalities, who have some unhealthy traits but are doing just fine. Some of these traits are the result of genetic factors, while others are mainly due to life experiences. It is important to realize that neither heredity nor environment have the final word about personality traits or styles. Most individuals, at least in our society, have an opportunity to shape their own personality and to lead healthier and happier lives. It is not easy to overrule our genes, but it has been done throughout human history."

Individuals with unhealthy personality styles *habitually* behave in an unrealistic, irrational, and/or negative manner; create intrapersonal or interpersonal discomfort or conflict; and/or, prevent others from attaining their full potential or enjoying their life. If we meet only one of these criteria, it will not be difficult to identify with one or more of the unhealthy personality styles described in this book.

An unhealthy personality style is a source of much personal and interpersonal discomfort. It makes us, or others, feel uncomfortable or uneasy, but it does not, for example, prevent us from doing responsible work, earning a living, attending school, or living independently. Even with an unhealthy personality style, we can still function pretty much like other individuals in our society. We are functional.

What Is a Personality Disorder?

A personality disorder is a major source of personal and/or interpersonal distress and impairment. We may find, for example, that we *cannot,* or *will not*: earn our own livelihood; live by ourselves; get along with others; safely drive a car; make sound decisions; trust other persons; obey the law; throw anything away; protect our physical, emotional, and spiritual health, and/or have guilt feelings.

The following is the definition of a personality disorder by the American Psychiatric Association (DSM-IV, APA 1994):

> A Personality Disorder is an enduring pattern of inner experiences and behavior that deviates markedly from the expectations of the individual's culture, is pervasive and inflexible, has an onset in adolescence or early childhood, is stable over time, and leads to distress and impairment.

Obviously there is a major difference between having a few unhealthy personality *traits* (which involves no significant discomfort for ourselves or others), an unhealthy personality *style* (which involves significant discomfort for ourselves or others), or, a personality *disorder* (which involves anguish and diminished abilities). Those who have a personality disorder usually lack insight into their problems, are closed to suggestions for personal change, and rigidly persist in distressful and dysfunctional ways.

It is important to recognize that many other important variables must be considered before a diagnosis of a personality disorder can be made. Only trained mental health professionals are in a position to make such a diagnosis. Thankfully, most of us only have some scattered unhealthy personality traits or perhaps one or more unhealthy personality styles. The latter is the focus of this chapter. Let's now look (in alphabetical order) at some common unhealthy personality styles.

Some Aspects of Unhealthy Personality Styles

The Antisocial (Sociopathic) Personality Style

A Convincing But Deceitful and Uncaring Person

Antisocial (sociopathic) individuals lack a well-functioning conscience and do, for the most part, whatever they please without regard for others. They can, however, skillfully hide their lack of conscience and true empathy behind a deceptive facade of charming and gracious behaviors. Some of these individuals hold authoritarian functions in such diverse fields as business, criminal justice, government, law, politics, and even religion. But they might also readily be found among those in *any* other occupation. Sociopathic persons are sexually exploitive, yet may present themselves as leaders in the forefront of teaching others how to be moral and faithful. The so-called predators we sometimes find in churches, or elsewhere, often have antisocial personalities. It is noteworthy that these individuals have invaded the church from the earliest days.

Although sociopathic individuals are oppressive and exploitive, they usually present themselves as cooperative, helpful, and kind, while secretly preparing to take advantage of unwary and vulnerable persons. They believe that others deserve to be taken advantage of because they see them as stupid. Caring only for themselves, sociopathic persons may fake social interests, but in reality are socially insensitive. They do not hesitate to violate the rights or well-being of others and will do anything to gain the upper hand over them.

Most of these individuals are masters of deceit and romantic persuasion. Deviant, impulsive, and irresponsible, they will callously go after whatever and whomever they want. They seek immediate gratification for whatever needs they perceive to have and then cover their tracks with deception and lies.

Sociopathic individuals, like their narcissistic counterparts, have an irrational belief in their own superiority and are eager to manipulate, intimidate, and dominate. The latter are characteristic elements of the occult, and the exact opposite of what we find in true followers of Christ. Why do these individuals do what they do? Genetic, biological, and environmental factors have helped to shape their unhealthy personality style. Those who have an antisocial personality style, or any other unhealthy personality style, can learn to have a healthy personality and renewed mind, as described in the remaining chapters of this book.

The Avoidant Personality Style

A Polite but Hypersensitive and Withdrawn Person

Avoidant persons are driven by well-hidden powerful fears. They are afraid that others may evaluate them negatively and are hypersensitive to humiliation, shame, or rejection. Oversensitivity and hypervigilance induce them to easily overreact to minor slights and innocent events and to become aversive to social interactions. Avoidant persons prefer to stay in the background and have well-established routines. Family ties are very important, and home is the center of their life. As creatures of habit, avoidant persons do especially well at repetitive and routine tasks.

Outwardly, avoidant persons may appear cool, polite, and reserved, but inwardly, they are tense and forever on the alert for any possible danger. Only in familiar surroundings are their inhibitions lessened and do they become more relaxed. Outside of those surroundings, however, avoidant persons once again become aloof, self-conscious, and withdrawn. An avoidant person's hypersensitivity to criticism can make him or her hard to live with. Even the possibility of humiliation or rejection may be enough for a total withdrawal. Avoidant persons are sometimes a target for unscrupulous individuals who seek to manipulate an avoidant person's fear of humiliation, shame, and rejection.

When avoidant persons believe they are being rejected, they often withdraw into an emotional shell—they will "put up a wall." In actuality, however, they desire emotional closeness but will not be truly committed to a close relationship without numerous assurances that it is safe to do so. Their continued ruminations, and worrisome testing of others, often make relationships with avoidant persons difficult or nonproductive.

Some Aspects of Unhealthy Personality Styles

During times of excessive stress, the defenses of repression and suppression of avoidant persons may completely break down and result in emotional numbness and unresponsiveness. Somatic problems, such as migraines (including ocular migraines), temporary loss of vision or hearing, and/or gastrointestinal problems, are not uncommon. A coexisting compulsive, dependent, or paranoid personality style is at times present in those who have an avoidant personality style.

The Borderline Personality Style

A GREGARIOUS BUT CAPRICIOUS AND UNSTABLE PERSON

Individuals with borderline personalities have highly intense, unstable, uninhibited, and spontaneous interpersonal relationships. They have impulsive, self-defeating actions, and rapidly alternating high and low moods. There is, however, an extensive range of cognitive, emotional, and behavioral differences between individuals with this complex personality style. Some, for example, are able to hold responsible positions (physicians, lawyers, and so forth), whereas some are totally dependent on others for their care. There seems to be a disproportionate number of women with this personality style. The latter probably stems from the frequent emotional, physical, and sexual abuse of girls and women in our society.

These *stress-sensitive complex individuals* usually suffer from a preponderance of anger, rages, temper tantrums, and suicidal thoughts. They rarely have a clear sense of self and often don't know who they are, or, more accurately, where they fit in. Needless to say, they often don't know very precisely what they want, but most of them want "something" now. That something, nearly always, and, logically so, includes unconditional acceptance, respect, and understanding. Common among these stress-sensitive and love-hungry individuals is a tendency to feel empty, bored, or tense. Hence, they are usually looking for some kind of activity—some place to go—something to distract them from their unhappy thoughts and feelings.

Most noteworthy, perhaps, are their stormy interpersonal relationships. These virtually always involve issues over control, intimacy, or trust, and are steeped in a "catch–22." Borderline persons, for example, are forever looking for leadership. But because they are fearful of being controlled, they seek to lead (control) the leader. They crave intimacy but can enjoy this only as long as they have a sense of personal control over a relationship. That is one reason, I believe, why an intimate relationship with a borderline person may come to an immediate halt at the moment of marriage—the thought of losing more of an already fragile identity is too overwhelming! To those who have some insight into the complex nature of these long-suffering persons, it is all quite understandable. Even their frequently found addiction to fast driving or dislike of car seat belts is understandable (but not recommended!).

To ask a borderline person to trust others is perhaps asking too much. Far too many have learned that it might be foolish to trust anyone! In addition to issues of control, intimacy, and trust, there are many other variables that may set the stage for troublesome interpersonal relationships. Borderline persons, for example, have more than a fair share of thinking errors, faulty beliefs, mood swings, obsessiveness, impulsivity, and compulsivity. In the area of impulsivity alone, they often get into trouble with their eating, financial, or sexual behavior.

Any amount of stress may result in aggravating physical problems with allergies, TMJ pain, neck pain, low blood sugar, PMS, and gastrointestinal difficulties. Even very mild stress may result in sudden manifestations of anger, anxiety, and/or depression. When stress becomes too severe, some borderline persons may even experience brief psychotic episodes or want to instantly escape from their present environment.

Suffering from a frantic fear of abandonment, borderline persons are in constant need of reassurances, and, in one way or another, of being connected to others. As a rule, this puts an enormous strain on interpersonal relationships, especially marital ones. The latter can be typified as hot or cold, extremely demanding, dichotomous, manipulative, and unstable. Without professional intervention, some spouses of borderline persons develop codependent behaviors, guilt complexes, substance abuse problems, and other emotional or physical problems.

The Compulsive Personality Style

A Conscientious but Critical and Perfectionistic Person

Compulsive persons are usually well-disciplined, respected, and respectful. Their dedication, dependability, and reliability frequently inspire trust in others. Hardworking, honest, and loyal, compulsive persons are often the backbone of successful organizations. The compulsive personality has some advantages, but, regrettably, this falls short of the healthy personality. This is especially true when this personality *style* evolves into a personality *disorder*. In that case, what started as a desire for excellence becomes a demand for perfection.

Compulsive persons are driven. They are very afraid of failure and especially the humiliation they believe comes with this. It is anxiety, rather than vision, that drives most compulsive persons to do well; they are seeking acceptance, respect, safety, and security. Many of them have endured some form of hardship in childhood or adolescence. While some compulsive persons were poor and are now looking for security, others were treated unfairly and now hunger for acceptance and respect. Many other compulsive persons, however, were raised by overachieving parents who, wittingly or unwittingly, perhaps taught their children to equate success with respect. Needless to say, a fear of failure, humiliation, and rejection feeds on itself and only increases a relentless search for perfection.

Compulsive persons are overly conscientious, and usually examine things too deeply; analyzing every little detail. Everything has to be "just right." They are overly methodical and systematic in all they do and prefer to live by schedules, notebooks, calendars, and laptop computers. In spite of all their efforts, they, of course, remain fallible, and thus continue to make mistakes. The latter are often seen as disasters. In order to prevent these "disasters," compulsive persons may start to procrastinate (waiting for the right time), or they become more and more indecisive (searching for the right decision).

If not controlled, their procrastination and indecisiveness only gets worse, and it becomes more and more difficult to make decisions. As their intrapersonal conflicts deepen, so do their interpersonal difficulties. Many compulsive persons seem to be at war with themselves—tired, perhaps, of (what they perceive as) having to prove to others (maybe a parent or spouse) that they are good enough. Many of them, I believe, are conformers, not by choice, but by force of conscience. They may deeply resent having to conform, but do so at an unconscious level, and, hence, remain anxious. From time to time their hidden resentments may surface, and a compulsive person may display *intermittent angry explosiveness.*

While the many good traits of a compulsive personality are initially helpful in the world of work, the negative aspects will become increasingly bothersome, and "burn-out" will take its toll. Compulsive persons rarely have any leisure time. Driven by a need for efficiency and control, they live by rules that must be closely adhered to, not only by themselves, but also by others. Since other individuals continue to fall short, the external world looks less and less ideal to compulsive persons, and as a result, they become more and more critical and judgmental. And as their own devotion to work, overconcscientiousness, and perfectionism increases; so does their intolerance of others who seem to lack these attributes. At this point, anxiety, depression, insomnia, or other physical and emotional problems are apt to manifest themselves in the life of a compulsive person.

Marital relations nearly always suffer because compulsive persons find it difficult to directly express their affection for a spouse or other family members. They may be deeply in love but may not express this verbally. This is especially true when there is a strong fear of losing control over one's emotions. "I must control my emotions at all cost," is often a deeply ingrained, unchallenged belief. It is not uncommon to find a combination of the compulsive and dependent personality style.

Some Aspects of Unhealthy Personality Styles

Note: It is important to distinguish a compulsive personality (someone who is overly conforming, controlling, orderly, and perfectionistic) from someone who has an Obsessive Compulsive Disorder (as seen in persistently recurring troublesome intrusive thoughts and uncontrollable, repetitive urges).

The Dependent Personality Style

A Devoted but Insecure and Clinging Person

Dependent persons show a pattern of anxious over-reliance on others. Feeling inadequate to cope with the demands of everyday life, they focus their attentions primarily on someone else. They do this not only because they seek acceptance, affection, approval, and respect, but also for personal protection. Basic to this personality style is a pervasive fear of abandonment, rejection, or separation. Seeing themselves as unable to cope with the ordinary demands of life, dependent persons will submit themselves wholeheartedly to others, as long as they are taken care of.

Sometimes we find a very unhealthy over-submissiveness—a willingness to do things that are unrealistic or irrational, and even unethical or immoral. Here, however, the behavior is more indicative of a dependent personality *disorder*. A dependent person's well-learned neediness or helplessness usually dates back to childhood or adolescence and may have gradually developed into an inability to make decisions without a lot of assurance. Not only a fear of decision-making, and hence, personal responsibility, but also a misperceived lack of personal qualifications, creates a growing cycle of dependency from which it is often difficult to escape without professional help.

One of the more troublesome aspects of having a dependent personality is vulnerability to abuse. Afraid of abandonment, rejection, separation, loneliness, and isolation, and unsure of their loveability, dependent persons are often abused by unscrupulous persons. Some dependent persons may also find themselves entangled in relationships with paranoid persons who are looking for submissive partners, or by borderline persons who are hungry for love and safety. But such a relationship quickly gets into trouble, for both the dependent and borderline person lack self-confidence, look for guidance, and are afraid of abandonment. As the borderline person places increasing demands or accusations on the dependent person, the latter may come to suffer from guilt-induced agonies. Professional help is usually necessary to unravel these dynamics, and help those involved toward a happier and healthier life.

When dependent persons develop health problems or additional emotional difficulties, they tend to become even more clingy, passive, submissive, and timid. Already afraid of giving offense, and seeing themselves as needy and weak, they are now even more vulnerable for dysfunctional relationships. They may, however, try to ignore or cover up difficulties in their relationships. Dependent persons who enable others to continue with such unhealthy or dangerous practices as alcohol dependency, are sometimes referred to as codependent.

The Histrionic Personality Style

A ROMANTIC BUT DRAMATIC AND IMPULSIVE PERSON

Histrionic persons probably learned early in life that personal needs for safety and security are more readily satisfied by being attractive, charming, or needy. There are, however, also many individuals who are naturally gregarious, extroverted, socially-engaging, and lively. Their outgoing personality traits are part of an overall healthy personality.

Those with more dysfunctional backgrounds, however, may develop an interpersonal style, which is characterized by an excessive need for affection, attention, approval, praise, nurturance, and reassurance. The more these individuals lean toward a histrionic personality *disorder,* the more they will also display charming, dramatic, flamboyant, impulsive, manipulative, and, sometimes, seductive ways. The latter may be evident in their dress, general demeanor, and speech. Although highly skilled in repressing and suppressing unhappy feelings and memories, histrionic persons are sometimes

Some Aspects of Unhealthy Personality Styles

quite aware of the incongruence between their facade of joyful exuberance and inner doubts and fears.

Many histrionic persons are masterful at controlling or influencing others through pleasurable experiences, creating comical or tragic events, being talkative, or in other ways providing interesting or entertaining situations. Others may influence their environment with various forms of dependency, including illness. In group settings, histrionic persons feel uncomfortable unless they are the center of attention. Some may also use sexually seductive behaviors and enhanced physical appearance to attract attention to themselves. Those who have a histrionic personality disorder usually have shallow or labile emotions, are highly suggestible, and try to impress others with a style of speech that is often confusing and nearly always lacking in necessary detail.

As with many other personality styles or disorders, there are various histrionic subtypes. Those who seek to smooth over any and all interpersonal difficulties develop many codependent personality traits. More bothersome, others may have such sociopathic personality traits as aggressiveness and deceitfulness. Histrionic persons, while perhaps outwardly perceived as charming, and gregarious, may inwardly hide moodiness, hidden resentments, and shallowness. Combinations of mixed histrionic-antisocial, histrionic-dependent, or histrionic-narcissistic personality styles are common. Histrionic persons are often self-centered, lack introspective reflectiveness, and focus far too much on what others may see in them, rather than the many "well-done" things they might easily find within themselves.

The Narcissistic Personality Style

A CHARMING BUT EGOTISTICAL AND EXPLOITIVE PERSON

Narcissistic persons, like their histrionic counterparts, crave admiration, but even more so, they crave power, position, and prestige. These, they will relentlessly seek to obtain, even at someone else's expense. Why? Because they are entitled to do this! At least that is what they think. Narcissistic persons are hopelessly convinced that they are very special. They may speak of love and act very "sweet," but in reality, they are only in love with themselves, even with their own artificial sweetness. Absorbed with their own importance, they find it inconceivable that others might not want to be with them, or be just like them. Narcissistic persons are hypersensitive to any form of criticism, no matter how benign or constructive, and quickly become enraged (even if they do not always show this) over minor slights.

Earlier I mentioned that many individuals with an antisocial personality may be found in the world of politics, law, and even religion, but, the same can also be said for narcissistic persons. It is important to recognize that narcissistic persons have no genuine empathy for others. They merely pretend that they understand and care for someone else's point of view, feelings, or suffering. In actuality, they are indifferent to the pain suffered by others or the havoc they create in the lives of others. Always seeking "center stage," they are professional soloists who hate to be in subordinate positions. They would rather form their own club, group, or fellowship, than be under the leadership and supervision of others. They not only seek fame and fortune, but actually believe that they are entitled to do so because of their superior qualities.

Living in an illusory world, they may claim the right to do as they please. Narcissistic persons are, all too often, self-appointed and self-serving leaders who try to compensate for their lack of a true sense of personal worth. They may seek to overcome an imbalanced childhood, or unhappy adolescent experiences, that may have left them with pseudo self-esteem in adulthood. Narcissistic persons may exploit others in all areas of life, and it is no surprise that many of them are married to persons with dependent personalities. After all, narcissistic persons live to be admired, and taken care of. Others are to be submissive to them and to be grateful for that opportunity. A narcissistic personality style is often accompanied by an antisocial and/or borderline personality style.

Some Aspects of Unhealthy Personality Styles

The Negativistic Personality Style

AN AUTONOMOUS BUT OPPOSITIONAL AND VACILLATING PERSON

Negativistic persons are driven by contrary thoughts, beliefs, and feelings, which are most likely the result of contradictory or hurtful messages received in childhood. Skilled at repressing and suppressing their resentments and other negative feelings, they may outwardly appear agreeable, while inwardly they do not agree at all!

These individuals usually anticipate disappointment and expect to be embarrassed, humiliated, or rejected. Because of their own capriciousness—shifting from agreement to disagreement, hot to cold, friendly to sulking—they often create the fulfillment of their own prophecies. Forever alert that someone may "step on them," they are afraid to assert themselves and lack cooperativeness and intimacy. Seeing themselves as vulnerable to the control, demands, and intrusiveness of others, they strive fervently for autonomy and self-sufficiency. Outwardly submissive, but inwardly aggressive, it is no wonder that there are so many interpersonal problems with children, spouses, friends, and coworkers.

Negativistic persons rarely recognize that they are, all too often, the instigators of interpersonal difficulties. Regrettably, they see these difficulties merely as the proof that they had been looking for—others are to blame! They see themselves as the victims of bossy, demanding, or domineering individuals who are "always trying to control them." Some of the most sincere gestures of kindness by others may be interpreted as abusive or intrusive. Realistic, but minor, interpersonal problems are likely to be blown up out of all proportion and seen as entirely the fault of others. Negativistic persons readily feel victimized, will bitterly blame others, collect grievances, and live with a mental storehouse filled with resentments. Under pressure, these individuals may erupt in outbursts of hostility, scorn, or rage, or go into a deep depressive withdrawal.

They have one main strategy in life: resist others! Firmly convinced that their way is the best way, they frequently remind themselves not to be influenced by anyone. But since they primarily operate by sabotage and subterfuge, they give lip service, saying one thing, but meaning another. They make promises they don't keep and perhaps never intended to. They may profess to forgive those who make amends or ask to be forgiven, but in reality they neither forgive, nor forget.

Negativistic persons may have suffered in childhood from so-called Oppositional Defiant Disorder, and even at that time they rarely apologized for any misbehavior. If they did, it was usually a matter of expediency. In their hearts, whether as adolescents or adults, they remain the unbending and unyielding "innocent victims" of a controlling environment or "unjust society"—one they may wish to use, but not serve, and would much rather have nothing to do with. Thus, they may continue to resist everyday normal demands from others and frequently try to sabotage them. They usually have a critical spirit, judgmental attitude, pessimistic outlook, resentful vengeance, and stubborn obstinacy, all packaged in surface submissiveness. Persons with a negativistic personality style may sometimes also have an antisocial, avoidant, borderline, histrionic, or paranoid personality style.

The Paranoid Personality Style

A Protective but Hypervigilant and Suspicious Person

Paranoid persons are suspicious, supersensitive, secretive, self-righteous, hyper-vigilant, and emotionally restricted. They may not outwardly show that they have a deep-seated distrust of others but are constantly suspicious of possible abusive and malicious motives. They usually see themselves, however, as noble, righteous, or vulnerable persons who seek tranquillity. Most likely, early in life some unhappy events conditioned them to see other individuals as potential adversaries. Paranoid persons are not psychotic but are sometimes confused with those who suffer from *paranoia*, which is a *psychotic delusional disorder*. Under stress, or clever manipulation by sociopathic or narcissistic individuals, a paranoid

Some Aspects of Unhealthy Personality Styles

person may also develop a delusional disorder, but this is usually only of a temporary nature.

They may outwardly appear quite normal, or even pleasant. Their autonomous, moralistic, and private behavior often gives them an unwarranted aura of trustworthiness, and an even more unwarranted aura of self-confidence. Inwardly, however, those with paranoid personality styles are beset with hypersensitivity, suspiciousness, and a strong tendency to unjustifiably blame people. Indeed they are grandmasters of ascribing their own faults to others. By doing so, they keep their anxiety levels in check; are able to feel "at one" with others, punish them, or keep them at a safe distance.

We might be tempted to think of paranoid persons as dishonest, yet they are quite sincere. They have so-called "blind spots," known as scotomas, in their personality structure. They do not have any conscious awareness of this. By using the unconscious protective defense mechanisms of *repression* (what is personally unacceptable is kept out of awareness), or *projection* (what is personally unacceptable is externalized), they obliterate whatever is too painful for them.

At the conscious level of awareness, however, paranoid persons continue to find things wrong with others, and especially with those closest to them. It is a paranoid paradox, that the individuals they could trust (those who truly love them), they refuse to trust because they suspect ulterior motives. Those whom they should not trust (e.g. narcissistic and sociopathic persons), sooner or later, may "bamboozle" them.

Significant others (spouses, friends, or children) in a paranoid person's environment often become bewildered and depressed by the way they are treated. Sometimes they may even start seeing themselves at fault for the growing number of difficulties experienced with the paranoid person—especially when that person drops his or her guard and openly shows suspiciousness, coupled with anger, bitterness, hatefulness, and outright malice. As a result, significant others are often at risk for emotional and/or physical problems.

Why is there all of this trouble in the first place? Self-fulfilling prophecy! Paranoid persons expect to be insulted, mistreated, or taken advantage of. They are on a perpetual collision course with other individuals. Without proper intervention, paranoid persons will become more and more isolated and secretive and convinced that they are being harassed, hassled, stalked, persecuted, or victimized in some other way.

They are forever wearing masks. We may find an aloofness in their facial characteristics and a weariness in their eyes, but it remains difficult to spot a paranoid person. Outwardly, they may appear cooperative, friendly, helpful, kind, and polite, while inwardly, they can be angry, critical, fault-finding, guarded, irritable, and/or resentful, all with polite restraint. They closely observe others, carefully weigh their own words, and try to present themselves in a beguiling manner. Paranoid individuals are found in all occupational, cultural, social, and religious settings, including Christian ministries and churches. It is estimated that there are at least one million, and perhaps as many as six million, individuals in this country with a paranoid personality disorder and far more with a paranoid personality style.

Paranoid persons are apt to question the fidelity of a friend or spouse and to see threatening things in some of the most harmless events. As grudge-bearing fault-finders, they often devise ways to test others in order to uncover possible evil or pretense. When all of that fails, they may skillfully create the very conditions that will provoke others to do exactly what they expected them to do. Thankfully, paranoid persons, like others with unhealthy personalities, can be helped to develop a healthier personality style, but it requires a lot of desire, effort, and patience. The biggest challenge to overcome is, of course, lack of insight. Paranoid persons are utterly convinced there is nothing wrong with them, and, consequently, they very rarely seek help.

Paranoid persons see themselves and their (usually over-protected) children, as victims, and will rarely compromise when facing interpersonal or marital problems. They are far more likely to accuse and attack than to look for a resolution of conflict. Most paranoid persons continue to live in a world "filled with potentially abusive, intruding, malicious, and oppressive individuals." A paranoid personality style can coexist with an avoidant, compulsive, narcissistic, or negativistic one.

The Schizoid Personality Style

AN UNOBTRUSIVE BUT DETACHED AND UNSOCIABLE PERSON

Schizoid persons may or may not function well in our society. Some are quite insightful and highly productive. Unofficially known as "loners," they neither desire, nor feel comfortable, with closeness. Because of their detachedness, they are not as beset by interpersonal conflicts as their more socially and emotionally involved counterparts. As a result, schizoid persons can freely give their energies to their special interest in business, industry, research, or science, and the pursuit of those hobbies or sports they can do by themselves.

Individuals with this personality style may, surprisingly, include directors of corporations, musicians, and school teachers, or have other occupations where they are in regular contact with, but not emotionally close to, others. Most of them, however, prefer solitary occupations, such as carpentry, bookkeeping, farming, or long-distance trucking. Impassive, and detached in social settings, they may seem aloof, quiet, withdrawn, or unsocial. Some, however, are just as skillful as negativistic persons in presenting an outward appearance that does not match their inward disposition. They may present themselves, for example, as outgoing and jovial individuals, and yet have no emotional involvement. These individuals have simply learned to outwardly respond to the emotive feelings of individuals around them.

Many schizoid persons have opted for a world of their own making—one that is less problematic than the one they grew up in. Although they are loners, they often do get married. It is here, however, that they meet their biggest challenge, if not their undoing. Sooner or later, their loner personality style surfaces and many problems may ensue. This is especially so because schizoid persons often have spouses with personality styles that are quite the opposite of their own. They are likely to marry those who see themselves as helpless and inept (*dependent*), confused and uncertain (*borderline*), self-sufficient and vulnerable (*negativistic*), impressive and gregarious (*histrionic*), or autonomous and superior (*sociopathic*). These vulnerable and unsuspecting individuals, with unhealthy personality styles of their own, are initially attracted to what they see as a capable, private, and/or quiet person—someone they believe they can trust, rely on, and get along with. Unhappily, none of the above mentioned personality styles mix very well with a schizoid personality style. A person with a schizoid personality style or disorder, at times, also has a coexisting avoidant, compulsive, dependent, or negativistic personality style.

Other Unhealthy Personality Styles

In the foregoing pages, I have presented the ten most common and best-known unhealthy personality styles. These unhealthy personality styles often exist in combination with other unhealthy personality styles. A person might, for example, have an avoidant-paranoid mixed personality style. Here the avoidant style is the dominant one, and the paranoid style is the less dominant one. But, it is also possible, and quite common, for a person to have two, or even three, unhealthy personality styles; for example, an avoidant and compulsive personality, or a borderline, histrionic, and narcissistic personality. It is also possible to have a certain personality style plus a few traits of other personality styles; for example, a negativistic personality with avoidant and paranoid traits. Here are a few additional unhealthy personality styles I should at least mention in passing.

The Depressive Personality Style

This personality style is sometimes found in individuals who have pervasive depressive personality traits, rather than depression or depressive illness. Unlike the real or perceived more recent losses found in depression, or the brain chemistry involvement found in depressive illness, we find mental fixations in depressive personalities. The latter have a long history of depressive thoughts, feelings, and behaviors. Regardless of their personal or social circumstances, depressive persons are nearly always cheerless, joyless, or unhappy. Devoid of a real sense of humor, they lead uninteresting and serious lives, and are at risk for stress-related illnesses. No matter what, these individuals have a negative point of view about the past, and are full of guilt, pessimism, remorse, restlessness, seriousness, self-blame, self-pity, and/or worry.

The Self-Defeating Personality Style

All human beings, from time to time, do some things that are self-defeating. Consciously or unconsciously, we occasionally sabotage ourselves. Self-defeating persons, however, turn self-sabotage into a lifestyle of self-inflicted misery. These individuals are so given to suffering as a way of life, that they seem dissatisfied unless there is something to be aggrieved about. They seem to feel insecure or unwanted unless they are weighed down with burdens—their own, or those of others. Their anxiety levels are perhaps reduced when they are "suffering." They may also assume that those who suffer much will be loved much. At times, some self-defeating persons purposely get into trouble and then bravely take their "deserved" punishment from a loved one and perhaps receive some hoped-for attention.

Some self-defeating persons seem bent on getting themselves into trouble. They may do whatever it takes to undo whatever good they have achieved. Other self-defeating persons may seek to be so self-sacrificing that others will be permanently indebted to them and, hence, provide them with real or imagined approval, affection, safety, and/or security.

The self-defeating person, in one way or another, however, seeks to have some kind of control over others. Whether through self-abasing, suffering, or sacrificing, there remains, of course, an element of personal choice. Self-defeating persons who choose to suffer or serve may thus obtain a sense of internal or external control. Many of these individuals, however, will go through life complaining or self-aggrandizing: "Look at me," they seem to say, "How I am mistreated," or "How unselfishly wonderful I am." The more objective observer, however, may find a rather difficult person who is given to criticizing and complaining with self-abasing, self-defeating, self-demeaning, self-sacrificing, and self-victimizing behaviors, but none of this is truly selfless! In short, the self-defeating person focuses on failure rather than success—on defeat rather than victory.

How to Overcome Unhealthy Personality Styles

Where do we go from here? Talking about different personalities is perhaps interesting, but more important is understanding what we can do to have a healthier personality style. Most of us have a choice as to what kind of person we want to be.

Some individuals are, of course, more vulnerable and may find it more difficult to make necessary changes. We need to remember that personality styles are the outcome of many complex biological, psychological, sociological, and spiritual factors. No human being at birth, during childhood, or adolescence puts in a request for a specific personality style. There are solid reasons behind the formation of every personality that exists. But whatever these reasons are, we must take courage in the fact that God loves us *all*, and that Christ died for us *all*. We must also be forever mindful that we can be overcomers in Christ. The Scriptures teach, and history confirms, that regardless of our past or present circumstances, we can change. In the next chapter, we will look at this in further detail.

13

BUILDING A HEALTHY PERSONALITY STYLE

My son, preserve sound judgment and discernment, do not let them out of your sight; they will be life for you, an ornament to grace your neck.

—Prov. 3:21–22

The more obvious aspects of a healthy personality consist of insight, openness, and flexibility—"sound judgment and discernment." These are typically found in individuals who live realistic, reasonable, and optimistic lives. A healthy personality does not just happen and is not a luxury. God wants us to choose freely and rationally. Only those, however, who can apply realism, reason, and optimism make wise choices. During the past decades, a growing number of researchers were justifiably excited as they discovered a direct link between personality and health. Their findings, however, only confirmed what believers learned long ago from scriptures that are thousands of years old. For example, the book of Proverbs reminds us of a direct link between our thoughts and our physical *and* spiritual health (Prov. 14:30; 16:24; 17:22; 18:21).

Researchers have also found that stressful events do not cause us to suffer from emotional or physical problems, but rather, our reaction, to these events. They learned that genes, biochemistry, and early childhood experiences are not the final determinants of happiness, wellness, or success in life. The final determinants are found in the incredible power of our mind—a mind which can be either a healer or a slayer. Our mind is solidly tied to our physical, emotional, and spiritual life. It is fascinating to see how brain chemicals directly influence our cognitions, emotions, memory, and day-to-day behavior, but we must remember that these chemicals, in turn, depend on a well-functioning body. It is important to recognize that a well-functioning body depends primarily on a healthy lifestyle!

If a healthy personality is essential for a healthy emotional, physical, and spiritual life, what can we do to have such a personality? An immediate answer that might "pop" into our mind would be: "Listen to God and repent." That most certainly would be the correct and most important decision of our life. It definitely would set us in the right direction. After all, in sincere repentance we readily acknowledge both our innate sinfulness and whatever sins we have personally committed. Deeply ashamed, grieved, and sorrowful for our past failures, we not only confess our sins, but wholeheartedly and zealously start working on a more sanctified life. It is completely true, of course, that we must "listen to God and repent," but it is equally true that, after repentance, we are to root out strongholds standing in the way of a sanctified life, including all unhealthy thoughts, feelings, and behaviors.

To have a healthy personality, we need to replace unhealthy personality traits with healthy ones. We need to start with habitually using realistic, reasonable, and optimistic thoughts and beliefs. It is not, however, the occasional constructive thought or belief that will bring us victory. What we need is consistent daily practice.

The Three Main Characteristics of Healthy Personalities

A healthy personality is not something that just happens. It takes desire and effort to achieve a healthy personality. "What is," we may rightly ask, "a healthy personality?" A person with a healthy personality is habitually *adaptable, caring,* and *constructive.* I would like to briefly describe this person.

Healthy Personalities Are Adaptable

An Adaptable Person is Insightful

One of the more blessed gifts a human being can have is the ability to perceive and interpret facts and events as objectively as possible. My own findings are that this ability is directly influenced by such factors as age, gender, and education. Insight, or self-understanding, refers to our ability to accurately observe and interpret our motivations and actions. Such self-understanding may require a courageous in-depth look at ourselves—courageous because we may have to deal with unpleasant issues or other things that we would rather repress or suppress; in-depth, because we need to have a thorough knowledge of all that "makes us tick." Adaptable persons are interested in objective reality; they want to live by facts, not illusions. Insight is essential if we are to adapt, or adjust, to the multifaceted and changing demands of life; it makes us aware of both our strengths and weaknesses and better prepared to make wise choices.

An Adaptable Person is Open-Minded

An adaptable person is always sincerely ready to consider the opinions of others. It is a sign of maturity if we can recognize our fallibility, admit that we might be mistaken in our observations or interpretations, and, if appropriate, yield to another point of view. Adaptable persons are open to suggestions and opportunities for constructive personal change. Recognizing that they "know and see in part," they are very responsive to new information, innovations, and technological advancements. Adaptable persons are willing to learn new and better ways, expand their bank of knowledge, and include others into their widening circle of friends.

AN ADAPTABLE PERSON IS FLEXIBLE

The ability to give or take, lead or follow, speak or listen, are just a few examples of the flexibility we find in adaptable persons. More importantly, perhaps, is their ability to adapt to great challenges, major changes, strong demands, or unhappy events that may suddenly come into their lives. What is noticeable about adaptable persons is that they accept unpleasant situations without anger, bitterness, or resentment. Within ethical boundaries, they are quick to cooperate, and, if necessary, to compromise. Adaptable persons don't have to win every game, debate, or race. Everything does not have to go their way. When circumstances dictate, they can readily lead, willingly follow, and gladly bend.

Healthy Personalities Are Caring

A CARING PERSON SHARES

In contrast to a pervasive preoccupation with self, which is so often found in those who have an unhealthy personality style, we find that healthy personalities are very caring persons. They like to share their blessings with others, not out of a sense of duty, nor a need for recognition or fame, but out of the fullness of their social conscience. Caring persons share their lives with others because they have a reverence for human life, the ability to look above and beyond themselves, and a sincere desire to minister to the needs of others. A caring person is altruistic, compassionate, empathetic, helpful, generous, and cares for the common good.

A CARING PERSON FORGIVES

Caring persons do not harbor anger, bitterness, hate, or resentment. They are quick to forgive those who make amends and seek pardon, or to bury their resentments when forgiveness has not been requested or is not possible for some other reason. Caring persons seek only what is good for others. They try to further the happiness and well-being of those they care for. They look ahead and not back; seek to build and not destroy. By forgiving others or burying their resentments, caring persons not only provide emotional relief to others, but they also free themselves from the unhealthy stress of unforgiveness or ongoing resentment.

A Caring Person Loves

Caring persons love others. I am not only talking about sincere feelings of affection or a devoted attachment to some special person or persons. I am also thinking about the full acceptance (happy welcoming) of other individuals, regardless of their educational, economic, social, racial, or other background, as well as deeply respecting others—that is, to not have bias or prejudice towards them. Caring persons accept, respect, and understand others from the objective perspective that all human beings are fallible and imperfect; that all human beings have one overriding, universal need—selfless love.

Healthy Personalities Are Constructive

Those who have healthy personalities live by *constructive thinking*— a composite of realistic, rational, and optimistic thinking. These mental elements are similar to those we find in Christian overcomers who live by truth, reason, faith, and love. This will be discussed in more detail in the final chapter. Here, however, we must focus on the three primary traits found in all healthy personalities (believers and unbelievers alike), namely realism, reason, and optimism.

Constructive Persons are Realistic

"Realistic thinking," I have stated elsewhere, "is synonymous with factual thinking; that is, the representation of objects and life as they really are. Realistic thinking focuses on the requirements of an external situation, is productive, and aids problem solving. Realistic thinking is concrete, practical, and real, and consequently is marked by its nonspeculative nature, dealing with facts rather than assumptions" (Brandt, 1988).

Realistic persons learn to question the accuracy of their perceptions and cognitions, and may check and double check them when making important decisions. These individuals learn to make a clear distinction between thoughts and feelings. They recognize that thoughts are mental elements, whereas feelings are physical/emotional elements. We think with our mind but feel with our body. Realistic persons also separate facts from fiction and knowledge from assumption. They don't believe everything they hear from others, or even from themselves. They frequently check on the accuracy of their perceptions, for example, when angry, anxious, or depressed. Realistic thinking is important if we seek to have insight.

Constructive Persons are Reasonable

To live by reason is to live by true and clear principles. Reason is the indispensable "glue" of a healthy civilization, whereas its absence is at the heart of a decaying one. The ability to reason, among other things, clearly sets human beings apart from the so-called animal kingdom. We are the only living creatures who have the ability of deducing one proposition from another or in finding intermediate ideas to connect distant ones. Without this ability, there is no human civilization, progress, future, or hope.

Reasonable persons seek, analytically and logically, to validate their cognitions, feelings, and actions. Reason helps them to improve their lives, achieve their goals, have appropriate emotions, and stay out of unwanted troubles. The absence of reason results in unhealthy lifestyles and untimely deaths for millions of individuals in this country. It is also responsible for widespread emotionalism, fanaticism, hedonism, narcissism, and other unhealthy personal and social manifestations. Those who embrace reason, however, seek to stay alive as long and as happily as possible, preserve their health, achieve their goals, have positive emotive feelings, and enjoy healthy interpersonal relationships.

How we reason literally determines how we feel. Most individuals like to feel calm, happy, tranquil, and at peace with themselves and others. Yet very few seem to know that their emotive feelings are mainly self-created. While our environment may provide the sources (circumstances and conditions), we provide the responses. We are in control of our feelings because we are in control of our thoughts, beliefs, and attitudes (no one can do this for us!). Our ability to reason helps us make wise choices and is the key to preventing significant conflict with others. Rational thinking is important if we seek to be open-minded.

CONSTRUCTIVE PERSONS ARE OPTIMISTIC

Over the centuries, there have been many individuals who believed that they lived in the best possible environment here on earth. They believed that, apart from heaven, a better world was not possible; everything in nature was as it should be; things were just fine. Even today, many persons might say that everything is indeed ordered for the best. Things are as they should be—the exact outcome of specific prerequisites. Constructive persons, however, habitually look for, and definitely expect to find, the very best in all circumstances of life; but, please note carefully, only in those circumstances that have first been realistically validated and rationally evaluated. In constructive thinking, we find that realism, reason, and optimism, go hand-in-hand together. Realism is clearly the foundation of constructive thinking, and reason is its structure, but optimism is the glue that holds it all together. To be a constructive person, and to have a healthy personality, we need all three elements.

If we lack optimism, we can be the most realistic or rational person in the world, and yet have a drab life, devoid of happiness, wellness, or success. As we look at even realistic or rational individuals in our environment, we may notice that some of them don't have a spark in their eye, a spring in their step, a smile on their face, or conviction in their voice. If we look more closely, we may discover that these individuals lack optimism—that confident and expectant belief, whereby human beings seek to find the very best in every situation. Optimism, the hopeful view that good things are going to happen, is not a luxury; it is essential for our physical and mental health, is stress-reductive, bolsters our courage, and boosts our immune system.

Constructive persons have a lot of optimism. It motivates them into action with confidence, calmness, and surety. These individuals expect that in the end all will be well. As Christians, we are reminded that in the end all is more than well, as the "last enemy, even death" is destroyed by Christ (cf. 1 Cor. 15:21–28). Optimism has many important tasks to perform in our lives—it helps us tackle tasks with eagerness, be more creative, imaginative, and stronger in spirit, mind, and body. Optimism is very good medicine. It is important, however, to not confuse optimism (positive thinking) with faith. The latter is a gift from God, while optimism is only a learned, helpful trait. It must be clearly understood that no amount of optimistic or positive thinking can *save* (deliver), *purify* (clean), *justify* (absolve), or *sanctify* (deliver) us. It is only through grace and faith that these events can take place. Nevertheless, it is true that all constructive persons have an optimistic frame of reference.

Other Characteristics of Healthy Personalities

Healthy personalities are adaptable, caring, and constructive, however, in addition to these three primary characteristics they may have as many as fifty secondary healthy personality traits. We may find, for example, that they are also assertive, compassionate, conscientious, courteous, disciplined, faithful, humble, humorous, modest, moral, polite, prudent, responsible, tactful, trustworthy, and so forth. Regrettably, it goes far beyond the scope of this chapter to discuss these traits in detail.

There is, however, one particular characteristic that we should look at. As we observe individuals with healthy personalities, we notice that they feel quite comfortable with themselves, other individuals, and life in general. This characteristic is the primary outcome, a very noticeable one, of the sound judgment and discernment we find in those who have healthy personalities. Let's briefly look at this phenomenon.

Healthy Personalities Are Comfortable

COMFORTABLE PERSONS FEEL GOOD ABOUT THEMSELVES

Comfortable persons are "chilled out." They don't make a lot of fuss over every petty issue, are not easily offended, don't feel quickly slighted, and don't have to stick to rigorous legalistic routines. Comfortable persons are content, satisfied, and at peace with themselves—not because they see themselves as good, special, or better than others, but by accepting the fact that they are fallible human beings, and recognizing that it is unrealistic and irrational to demand perfection in their own or anyone else's life.

Those who feel comfortable with themselves are able to deal, to their satisfaction, with the many conflicting factors (such as needs and desires versus realities) within themselves or their environment. They refrain from placing unrealistic or irrational demands on themselves and set realistic goals. These individuals can laugh at themselves and will readily admit that they are imperfect. They recognize that their power of choice is sometimes limited by genetic, biochemical, or other factors. Yet, they accept full responsibility for their own emotional life. Comfortable persons are content.

COMFORTABLE PERSONS FEEL GOOD ABOUT OTHERS

Comfortable persons take for granted that others get along with them, even like or love them, but, unlike so many with unhealthy personality traits, they never insist that others "should" or "must" do so. Those who are at peace with others neither criticize nor seek to control them. Instead, they are objective and patient listeners, readily communicate on both a verbal and nonverbal level, and respect the cultural and other differences they may find.

Comfortable persons gladly and cheerfully support others, console them, lessen their distress, enhance their well-being, and further their happiness, wellness, and success. They are able to associate, cooperate, and form friendships with individuals of different backgrounds without necessarily endorsing all of their beliefs, values, or behaviors. Above all, they are free from any urge to control, overpower, or punish other individuals.

COMFORTABLE PERSONS FEEL GOOD ABOUT OBJECTIVE REALITY

Comfortable persons feel content, satisfied, and secure. This is quite different than being aloof, dispassionate, or withdrawn—these are unhealthy traits. Comfortable persons actively and wholeheartedly seek to alter or overcome unpleasant or harmful conditions but do so without dysfunctional anger, anxiety, or depression. They accept, as calmly as possible, that which cannot be changed. They see the world, in spite of its all-too-often chaotic appearance, as a place where nothing happens unless the necessary prerequisites have been met.

To be a comfortable person—at peace with self, other individuals, and the environment at large—is, from a Christian perspective, not necessarily enough and might even be a dangerous illusion. The reader is reminded at this point that the complete message of this book can only be found when the final page has been read. To be a comfortable person is only one aspect of a healthy personality, and the latter is only one aspect of a Christian personality. It is important to keep this in mind as we study this chapter.

Having said all of the above, we also need to recognize that there are many obstacles that make it more difficult for some persons to feel comfortable or have a healthy personality. We are mindful, for example, of such powerful obstacles as genetic encumbrances, negative childhood experiences, poor physical health, inadequate nutrition, unsatisfied needs, social injustices, and lack of opportunities.

Healthy Personalities Are Not Perfect

In this chapter, we have concluded that healthy personalities are adaptable, caring, and constructive. We also observed that healthy personalities feel comfortable about themselves, other individuals, and life in general. Clearly, there are tremendous advantages to having a healthy personality. It enables us to have more happiness, wellness, and success in our life. Even healthy personalities, however, remain fallible, imperfect, and sinful persons. We are liable to fail, make errors, misjudge facts or events, and so forth. Worse, we are inclined to do wrong things and sometimes even violate God's standards. Healthy personalities are definitely not perfect and cannot be perfect.

As stated before, there is a major difference between believers with healthy personalities and unbelievers with healthy personali-

Building a Healthy Personality Style

ties. Believers, for example, rely heavily on God for that which they cannot accomplish on their own: "He will call upon me, and I will answer him; I will be with him in trouble, I will deliver him, and honor him." (Ps. 91:15; also see John 12:26 and Rom. 8:37). Unhappily, there are far too many believers who have decidedly unhealthy personalities and are causing much harm to others and themselves. Some may think it impossible that a born-again Christian can still be in bondage to unrealistic, unreasonable, and/or negative personality traits. Not only is it possible, it's an everyday fact of life.

The Bible urges *believers* to acquire a renewed mind and transformed life: "Therefore, I urge you, brothers . . . be transformed by the renewing of your mind . . ." (Rom. 12: 1,2). In my work and studies, I have concluded that believers who are interested in having a renewed mind and transformed life may benefit greatly from taking a closer look at their personality style and its connection to a healthy physical, mental, emotional, and spiritual life.

Having considered several aspects of the healthy personality (one we hope to find in believers and unbelievers alike), we are getting closer to taking a look at the Christian personality. First, however, we need to briefly consider the subject of happiness. What is the secret of happiness? We are about to find out!

14

THE SECRET OF HAPPINESS

> But may the righteous be glad and rejoice before God; may they be happy and joyful.
> —Ps. 68:3

Everything that human beings do is in one way or another tied to the pursuit of happiness. I am not saying that this is necessarily a good thing. But every person I have ever met, whether professionally or socially, without exception, wanted to have a happy life. Throughout history there have been numerous scholars who have looked closely at the subject of happiness. Interestingly, they have never been able to agree on a universally acceptable description or definition of happiness. Happiness, it seems, is one thing to one person and another thing to another person. Many individuals, however, do agree that happiness is a matter of spirit, mind, and body. We experience happiness on a spiritual, intellectual, and "feeling" level. Since these events depend on functional and organic elements of the brain, we may conclude that happiness is a choice for most individuals.

Is Happiness a Choice?

Not always. There are hundreds of books, and thousands of articles, that seek to convince more or less unsuspecting readers how to harness happiness. Much of the advice, however, whether of a secular or religious nature, merely reflects compartmentalized advice. Compartmentalized, because it fails to take the total person and his or her unique circumstances into account. Compartmentalized, because it addresses either spiritual, mental, emotional, social, or physical aspects of happiness. All too often, this leads to seemingly easy, but incorrect, advice. Take the frequently heard statement that "happiness is a choice." While happiness is a choice for most individuals (at least in our society), it is completely wrong to say that happiness is always a choice.

To choose happiness, we need to have a functioning brain, a certain amount of intellectual ability, education, training, information, and so forth. Millions of individuals with seriously impaired brain chemistry find it very difficult, and at times impossible, to be happy. We must be careful, for example, not to unwittingly imply that individuals with serious genetic problems, brain trauma, or major biochemical imbalances, can simply choose happiness. It is even worse, of course, if we blame their unhappiness on an alleged failure on their part to choose wisely.

Happiness is obviously not simply a choice for everyone. Those who think so, need to consider those living in hospitals, nursing homes, concentration camps, and prisons; the emotionally, physically, and sexually abused; the hungry and the starving, and others in dire straights. It is, of course, ridiculous to think that those with Alzheimer's, or other neurological disorders, can simply choose to be happy. And dare we assume that the multiple millions of individuals who have been seriously traumatized by so-called ethnic cleansing, hate crimes, racial injustice, war, and scores of other devastating atrocities, have the same window of opportunity to choose happiness as those who have been deeply loved, closely protected, and safely sheltered all of their life? Certainly no rational person believes that those individuals who are begging for a drink of water or a small morsel to eat and who are literally starving to death (forty-thousand starve to death every day), ought to be reminded that happiness is a choice. I hope not.

Is All Happiness the Same?

Happiness, some modern gurus tell us, can strictly be found within ourselves, and we can choose to be happy even when things around us are really bad. Happiness, they insist, has nothing whatsoever to do with our circumstances or anything that is outside of ourselves. All we have to do, according to these "experts," is to simply go with the emotional flow that comes from within ourselves. Never mind, they seem to say, if we have unhealthy or healthy personalities, are well-fed or starving, if our chemistry is balanced, or if we live under some form of social, physical, emotional or spiritual bondage. All happiness, they imply, is just the same.

Happiness, they tell us, has nothing at all to do with choices, ethics, morals, religion, or values. In fact, those who teach these things believe that no action, direction, or effort of any kind, is required for human beings to be happy. They simply need to look within themselves. All of this go-with-the-flow, just-look-inside-yourself-and-forget-everything-else-stuff is pure nonsense. Worse, it is a lie about human happiness that is hard to catch, for it is embedded in partial truth.

It is, of course, true that most individuals in our society choose their own happiness. In fact, no one else can do this for them. If we believe that other individuals control our brain and, hence, our mind, then we are indeed in trouble. It is foolish to think that we cannot do anything about our own happiness. It is quite another matter, however, to believe that fallible, imperfect, sinful human beings only have to look within themselves to find everything they need for their happiness. Both saint and sinner would greatly fool themselves.

If happiness is only an undifferentiated feeling state that exists apart from our good or bad choices, then all happiness is the same. But all happiness is not the same. We can, for example, readily identify spiritual and worldly happiness. Before we look at this somewhat more closely, let's first consider happiness in general.

What Is Happiness?

Happiness, rightly or wrongly, means different things to different individuals. There are undoubtedly thousands of descriptions, definitions, and opinions on what happiness really is. In spite of this, many individuals would agree that happiness involves perceptions, cognitions, emotions, and behavior. And thus they might further agree that happiness is a *mental state* (e.g. peace of mind or contentment), an *emotive state* (e.g. pleasure or delight), and a *physical state* (e.g. biochemical events and behavioral expressions). Happiness, it seems, is a rather complex phenomenon, which impacts our mental, emotional, and physical life.

Happiness, from a Christian perspective, is more a point of view than anything else. Many Christians prefer, within the confines of modern language usage, to say that they feel *blessed*, rather than to say that they feel *happy*. Such a seemingly narrow distinction may not make much sense to some individuals, but it actually does convey an important insight. These Christians strongly believe that the common use of the word *happiness* does not always correctly describe their true sentiment of a lasting gratitude to God for past, present, *or* future blessings. They want to make a clear distinction between blessings as a mental state, and happiness as a feeling state. Even when temporary pleasure is absent, they can say with the apostle Paul: "For our light and momentary troubles are achieving for us an eternal glory that far outweighs them all. So we fix our eyes not on what is seen, but on what is unseen. For what is seen is temporary, but what is unseen is eternal" (2 Cor. 4:17).

Another point of view, one which is perhaps shared by many individuals, is that we need to be careful that our emotions do not turn into emotionalism—the practice of placing subjective experiences ahead of objective observations. Emotionalism is, of course, the antithesis to reasonableness, and often, of truth itself. All too many individuals are persuaded to acquire the habit of emotional excitement in response to experiences they neither understand nor question. Emotionalism has led many individuals into false doctrine and the enslavement of cultism. God, however, does not appeal primarily to our emotions, but to our sensibilities and conscience; not to closed minds, but to open minds; not to feelings, but to facts (cf. Prov. 18:15; 1 John. 4:1; Gal. 6:7).

Happiness is best understood as a fairly steady or enduring frame of reference—a baseline, as it were. It's an attitude, rather than a convincing thought or a strong belief; more an internal point of view than an external manifestation; more a mood than an emotion. A mood is long-lasting and pervasive, coloring all aspects of our life, while an emotion is more fleeting, selective, and shallow. Happiness, I believe, needs to be separated from such less-enduring emotional states as cheerfulness, excitement, delight, gladness, fun, or pleasure.

Happiness may also be seen as a state of mind, where most of our needs and wishes are satisfied, or as the absence of discomfort. Of course, here we are, once again, reminded that happiness may well be in the eye of the beholder. What may give some individuals plenty of happiness (or, more accurately, what some individuals make themselves happy over), may give other individuals a lot of unhappiness. It is clearly important that we learn to distinguish between objective and subjective happiness—between what is true and what, perhaps, is false. Let's have a look.

FALSE HAPPINESS

There are plenty of individuals who are leading corrupt, destructive, immoral, selfish, or otherwise worldly lives, but who seem to be quite happy. Indeed, we can find all kinds of individuals who are involved with criminal or other unsavory activities who yet seem to live in a state of perpetual happiness. Some of their broadly-smiling faces can regularly be seen on magazine covers, television screens, and so forth.

It is especially easy for those who have certain unhealthy personality styles to have a false sense of happiness. Many narcissistic and sociopathic individuals, for example, enjoy false happiness in manipulating, intimidating, and dominating others. Many others have convinced themselves that their conniving, deceiving, exploitive, shameless, or superficial ways are fun. Having themselves been bamboozled by Satan, they now merrily bamboozle others. Unless they repent of their sins, meet and follow Jesus Christ—the Lord of happiness and the source of everything that is good—they will continue to live the lie that all happiness, regardless of what and whose they are, must be allowed to flow from within themselves. That lie I have often encountered in my professional work when someone exclaims, "But if it feels good, it has to be good," or, "It feels so good, I know it is right." They remind me of the many individuals in our confused and reckless society who are seeking happiness, wellness, and success at any cost. It is no wonder that many of them are finding their own particular brand of happiness in the dark, spiritual world of the occult. Satan and his demons will gladly provide them with "happiness"—a fraudulent and illusionary happiness. These bamboozled individuals never knew, or have forgotten, that Satan comes as an "angel of light." He is a consummate con artist!

Many, indeed, are the individuals who are engaged in worldly hedonistic activities. Their pursuit of happiness is pagan or neo-pagan, their dogma of pleasure is of the devil, and their eternal future is in great peril. Believing that self-indulgent sensual pleasure is the principal good in human life, they engage in the inordinate pursuit of pleasure in eating, drinking, gaming, sex, and so forth, in total disregard of God's wise directives and boundaries. When we look at the results of these pursuits—drunkenness, family breakups, health problems, car accidents, sexually transmitted diseases, poverty, and crime—we know that in following a neo-pagan, hedonistic lifestyle, people are passionately sawing off the tree branch they are sitting on.

TRUE HAPPINESS

True happiness, at least from a Christian perspective, is spiritual happiness, and this obviously does not automatically flow out of fallible, imperfect, and sinful human beings. To the contrary. In spite of thousands of years of civilization, many people brutalize and destroy their fellow human beings in ways that are impossible even for the most savage creature in the animal world. True happiness does not flow from abusive, sadistic, or similarly disordered individuals. It does not flow from self-centeredness, selfishness, ignorance, or stupidity. And it does not even flow from those who have a healthy personality and love style, unless they have been filled with the goodness that flows from God.

The end of man, says the old catechism, is to glorify God by enjoying Him and all that He gives us *forever*. Some might say that Christians must not place any emphasis on happiness, but such a view is not biblical. The problem with happiness, says C. S. Lewis, is not that our desire for happiness is too strong, but that it is too weak (*The Weight of Glory and Other Addresses,* C. S. Lewis, 1965). We may settle for too little happiness, rather than too much. True happiness, spiritual happiness, like the kingdom of God, is indeed to be within us, but it does not originate with us. Only after we have been filled with the pleasure of knowing God, and the manifold blessings that come with this, can we have and share happiness—not a happiness that we have given to ourselves, but a happiness that God has offered to us, and we have chosen to accept. Having looked about us, and having received an offer of blessings or curses, of life or death, we must wisely choose to forego false promises, subjective impressions, deceptions, lies, or illusions. Most of us can choose to make ourselves happy but must do so realistically and rationally. Happiness, we discover, is something that we must carefully consider and wisely choose.

How wonderful when our happiness has a "firm foundation"— the foundation of truth, reason, and faith. "This day," we read in Deuteronomy 30:19, "I call heaven and earth as witnesses against you that I have set before you life and death, blessings and curses. Now choose life. . . ." Neither God the Father, nor God the Son, nor God the Holy Spirit, force themselves on us. God chooses to make Himself known to us, but then in His own sovereign way, He wants us to yield that we may have life, and that abundantly. The happiness of the Christian believer is found in a true and lasting fellowship with Jesus Christ—the Lord of Lords, the King of Kings, the One and only true Happiness-Provider. The Christian's happiness is more than just a contented mental state because intellectual, emotional, physical, or social desires and wishes may have been satisfied. It is more than a pleasant emotive feeling, based on some biochemical event, or a health-promoting experience (cf. Prov. 16:24). Happiness for Christian believers is the blessed outcome of not only *hearing,* but also *doing,* the Word of God (Luke. 11:28; James 1:22). More than a century ago, Hanna Whitehall Smith (1952) stated so eloquently that it is the birthright of every child of God to be happy; to have a life of inward rest and outward victory. She spelled out in great detail that a Christian's happiness could only be found by overcoming evil habits, conquering sins, removing negative dispositions, renewing our minds, and transforming our lives. The only way, she explained, by which all of this could possibly be accomplished was by "yielding ourselves unto God, and our members as instruments of righteousness unto Him. . . ." What a far cry from the misbelief and false teachings that we don't have to do anything to be happy; just go with the flow! Our happiness and joy must have a sound foundation: "But may the righteous be glad and rejoice before God; may they be happy and joyful" (Ps. 68:3).

It is undoubtedly a sign of the times that so many persons are deluding themselves into false happiness based on frivolous, misleading, and sinful events. The pursuit of happiness, based on immorality, impurity, or greed, is a sure ticket to disaster. True happiness has to line up with "goodness, righteousness, and truth" (Eph. 5:9). This kind of happiness does not come from trusting our feelings, but from trusting God; not from what seems good, but from what is good; not from arbitrary inferences, but from facts. Only those who yield themselves completely to God, who trust Him with every aspect of life, will "rejoice before God" and be "happy and joyful."

True happiness does not just happen; it does not happen merely because we believe in God, go to church, speak in tongues, have great preaching skills, sing in the choir, or whatever else we may do, unless God's love is active in our lives. Of course, we can have a false sense of happiness by wrongly perceiving and erroneously interpreting that we have chosen the right direction, when in fact, we are going in the wrong direction (cf. Jonah). It is wise to always remember that fact comes before faith and feeling. When it comes to salvation and consecration, for example, we may not always feel that we have embraced them fully, if at all. Here it is important to remember that "faith comes from hearing the word of God," or as Hannah Whitehall Smith reminds us, "God's invariable rule in everything is fact first, faith second, and feeling last of all."

If we want to be sure that we have true happiness, we must look to God's Word. In the Scriptures, God reminds us that important aspects of happiness include *listening, trusting,* and *obeying* Him. God reminds us that happiness is an outcome; it flows from our active and obedient participation in His will. For example, those who have mercy on the poor, keep the law, and walk as "children of the light" will be happy. It's also a matter of sharing God's love. If we bless royally, we shall be rewarded royally (Luke 6:38). The scriptural prescription for happiness is clear: Seek the Kingdom of God, obediently yield yourself to God, trust Him fully, and you will experience the happiness of the righteous. The prescription for a long and lasting happiness is found in God's Word. Here is a scriptural happiness prescription for believers:

Rx for Happiness

Praise God from Morning till Night

> Praise the Lord, all you nations; extol him, all you peoples. (Ps. 117:1)

It is not possible to joyfully praise the Lord and at the same time be unhappy. This is well-demonstrated in Psalm 13:

> How long, O LORD? Will you forget me forever? How long will you hide your face from me? How long must I wrestle with my thoughts and every day have sorrow in my heart? How long will my enemy triumph over me? Look on me and answer, O LORD my God. Give light to my eyes, or I will sleep in death; my enemy will say "I have overcome him," and my foes will rejoice when I fall. But I trust in your unfailing love; my heart rejoices in your salvation. I will sing to the LORD, for he has been good to me.

Here is David, in the midst of his despair. He believes wrongly that God has forgotten him, complains about this, accuses God of hiding from him, pleads to be heard, and calls out to be rescued from his depression. But then a change takes place. David switches from lamenting his lot in life; from doubting and questioning he moves to trusting God. David changes his frame of reference. He starts to speak truth, reminds himself of God's mercy, and step-by-step, moves from despair to happiness.

Christians cannot focus on God's blessings and stay unhappy! The love of God *is* expressed in the gift of salvation, and even in the midst of hardships we can learn to sing again if we extol the blessings of God. Every time we say "Hallelujah," we say "praise the Lord," and are empowered by this. We are reminded throughout the Scriptures to praise God: "I will praise you, O LORD, with all my heart; I will tell of all your wonders. I will be glad and rejoice in you; I will sing praise to your name, O Most High" (Ps. 9:1,2).

Numerous indeed are the ways in which we can praise God—with prayer, song, church worship, mind, heart, and so forth. We must never neglect to speak of the goodness and mercy of God. The more we focus on the light and love of God, the less we focus on the darkness that may surround us. We praise God precisely for calling us out of darkness.

We are reminded that we are ". . . a chosen people, a royal priesthood, a holy nation, a people belonging to God, that you may declare the praises of him who called you out of darkness into his wonderful light" (1 Pet. 2:9). Let us praise God from morning till night and never cease to be grateful for His faithfulness toward us. Yes, the righteous will be glad and rejoice before God.

S<small>PEAK</small> O<small>NLY</small> W<small>HOLESOME</small> W<small>ORDS</small>

> Do not let any unwholesome talk come out of your mouths . . . (Eph. 4:29).

It is very easy for us to feel unhappy. All we have to do is think about some unhappy events or speak unhappy words. If we focus for just a few minutes on how "everything" is "always" going wrong for us, or that "no one loves us," we start feeling badly. For good mental health, and the prevention of negative emotions, it is important not to feel sorry for ourselves. Not only may negative "self-talk" lead to feelings of anger and depression, but it also hurts our relationships with others. God wants us to speak in ways which are ". . . helpful for building others up according to their needs, that it may benefit those who listen" (Eph. 4:29).

It is well known that self-pity, self-blame, and other blame are major sources of depression. Since feelings are the result of our perceptions and interpretations of facts or events, we must learn to live by truth, reason, and faith. To have peace of mind and true happiness, we need to think and speak about wholesome things (Phil. 4:4–8). Do we want to be happy? Then let's start with this: "Get rid of all bitterness, rage and anger, brawling and slander, along with every form of malice. Be kind and compassionate to one another, forgiving each other, just as in Christ God forgave you" (Eph. 4:31, 32).

Steadfastly Do Our Daily Tasks

> Commit to the Lord whatever you do, and your plans will succeed (Prov. 16:3).

When heavy burdens overwhelm us, and we fail to absorb the blueness of the sky or the greenness of the grass, we may not want to do even the slightest thing. Sometimes, however, we make things worse by telling ourselves that we cannot do anything, while in truth we can do many things, but we don't feel like doing them. And since feelings result from what we tell ourselves, it is only logical that we cannot do some of the simplest tasks. In my work, I have, on more than one occasion, seen how some persons talk themselves into immobility, but with some prodding were able to talk themselves into becoming mobile once again.

Sometimes it is useful to make a simple schedule of our daily tasks and to follow that schedule whether we feel like it or not.

The Renewed Mind

Rather than respond to our feelings, we respond to our wishes, as depicted in the schedule. Our daily tasks should also include mealtimes—the mind cannot function very well when the brain lacks nutrients. There are many reasons why we may not feel like doing anything, but perhaps we can overcome our inertia by realizing that to be an overcomer in Christ, we need something to overcome. Consider this: "These (trials) have come so that your faith—of greater worth than gold, which perishes even though refined by fire—may be proved genuine and may result in praise, glory and honor when Jesus Christ is revealed" (1 Pet. 1:7). Let us fully trust in the Lord.

Apply Our Talents

> Now we see but a poor reflection as in a mirror; then we shall see face to face. Now I know in part; then shall I know fully, even as I am fully known (1 Cor. 13:12).

The sooner we accept the fact that we see in part and know in part, the happier we will be. All of us share common limitations of fallibility and imperfection, but in addition, we have limitations that are specific to us. Some individuals have more limitations than others, but it remains folly to compare ourselves to others. It is in the will of God that we are different and that we use our talents well. Instead of focusing on limitations, we must focus on the strengths and talents that God has given us.

While all human beings have certain universal limitations, others have incredible burdens they can only carry with the help of the Lord Himself. Yet, look at such overcomers as Helen Keller, Corrie ten Boom, Joni Eareckson-Tada, Dave Roever, Joel Sonnenberg, and so many others. We must stop comparing ourselves to those who seem better off and start reaching out to those who are worse off than we are. Rather than dwelling on our handicaps, hardships, or limitations, we are to witness to others about the Great Comforter who has strengthened us and lifted us high above our afflictions, and who enables us to say with the apostle Paul: "Praise be to the

God and Father of our Lord Jesus Christ, the Father of compassion and the God of all comfort, who comforts us in all our troubles, so that we can comfort those in any trouble with the comfort we ourselves have received from God" (2 Cor. 1:3,4).

Have More Esteem For Others

> Why do you look at the speck of sawdust in your brother's eye and pay no attention to the plank in your own eye? (Matt. 7:3)

Apart from the fact that all human beings are fallible, imperfect, and sinful, we also find that they are different. For starters, they may have genetic backgrounds that predispose them to differences in ability, temperament, and personality. Next, they all have their own unique perceptual-cognitive field; their own distinct way of perceiving and interpreting the world around them. The latter is, of course, greatly influenced by education, training, and a multitude of other experiences. It is little wonder that no two individuals can experience anything in an absolutely identical manner. Yet, some of us keep insisting that others "should" perceive, think, feel, and act just as we do.

Although it is impossible to find even one perfect person on the face of this globe, we continue to upset ourselves over the imperfections of others. The more compulsive and perfectionistic we are, the greater the likelihood that we will find something wrong with other individuals. Worse, whenever someone fails at one thing or another, we are all too ready to place a global rating on that person. A student receives a low grade in a particular course and is rated a poor student; a person arrives late for work and is seen as a sluggard; someone does not quickly grasp what we are teaching and is called stupid. Many individuals foolishly also place global ratings on themselves; they fail at one thing or another and call themselves dumb, or even worthless.

As fallible human beings, we can be sure that sometimes we will fail; we will make errors, and we will sin. This insight, however, is not a license to do foolish things, much less to sin. Rather, its an urgent reminder not to do those things, and not only to refrain from judging others, but rather to esteem others better than ourselves (Phil. 2:3). It is legalism and selfish pride that makes us so frantic about the minor imperfections of others, while we fail to see our own need for more humility. It is foolish and self-centered to think that we can be utterly qualified, intelligent, and achieving in everything we do. Placing unrealistic and irrational demands on others, or on ourselves, is a sure ticket to unhappiness. It will leave us discontent, dissatisfied, and disheartened. Let us remember that God wants us to refrain from being judgmental of others and also of ourselves (1 Cor. 4:1–5). We must leave the assessment of our personal worth to God; He is faithful, and He will deliver us: "I sought the LORD, and he answered me; he delivered me from all my fears" (Ps. 34:4). Finally, let us never forget that "While we were still sinners, Christ died for us" (Rom. 5:8).

Forgive and Forget

> ". . . as far as the east is from the west, so far has he removed our transgressions from us (Ps.103:12)."

Blaming ourselves, whether for real or imagined failures, is not going to resolve any problems. Appropriate, constructive regret is one thing, but lamenting is rarely helpful. It is even worse when we irrationally insist that we should have done things differently. Of course, we would have done many things differently, if we could have known the future. Many, if not most, of the mistakes we made in the past had to happen. When we walk in darkness, we reap darkness. Emotional troubles, ignorance, stupidity, and many other variables may have contributed to our poor choices or errors in judgment. Perhaps we were unable to do better. But even if we were unwilling to do better, the fact remains that human fallibility and sinfulness are powerful forces that sometimes propel us into self-defeating behaviors. Every living human being has made mistakes and will make mistakes again.

As for our sins, God provides legal forgiveness to those who do not yet belong to the family of God if they acknowledge their sins, repent of them, and believe in Jesus Christ as the Son of God: "For God so loved the world that he gave his one and only Son, that whoever believes in him shall not perish but have eternal life" (John. 3:16). If we already belong to the family of God, but have failed in one way or another, then we obtain family forgiveness if we are truly sorry and confess these sins: "If we confess our sins, he is faithful and just and will forgive us our sins and purify us from all unrighteousness" (1 John. 1:9). And if we are guilty of hurting others, we must seek interpersonal forgiveness by being truly sorry, making restitution if at all possible, and asking for forgiveness (Matt. 6:14,15; 18:15-17, 23-35; Luke 3:8; 17:3; Acts. 26:20; Rom. 12:19-21).

Some individuals are willing to forgive others, but pride or some other hindrance prevents them from accepting either God's forgiveness, or the forgiveness of others. God is ready and willing to forgive our sins, but, strangely, some individuals see themselves perhaps even above God. Our Heavenly Father wants reconciliation between Himself and us and between others and ourselves. Happiness cannot come to us if we refuse to accept God's forgiveness or fail to forgive those who are sorry for their sins and seek our forgiveness. When God forgives us our sins, we are to look forward, not backward. We are to stop blaming and pretending that we can attain perfection here on earth: "Brothers, I do not consider myself yet to have taken hold of (perfection). But one thing I do: forgetting what is behind and straining toward what is ahead, I press on toward the goal to win the prize for which God has called me heavenward in Christ Jesus" (Phil. 3:13,14).

REACH OUT TO OTHERS IN LOVE

> "This is the message you heard from the beginning: We should love one another" (1 John. 3:11).

Happiness will remain elusive if we fail to love and be loved. We may never fully experience happiness unless we know that someone affectionately and selflessly cares for us, and we do likewise.

Such a selfless and lasting love relationship can only be found in a personal relationship with God. It is God who seeks us out and who offers His love to us. As we mature in the love of God, we will increasingly learn to love others affectionately and selflessly.

Love is the central dynamic in happiness. This is how I described some of my thoughts on this previously: "To love, therefore, is the ultimate in right thinking and right feeling. Although love is an emotion, it is far more than just an emotion. Love is also thought and action. For to love as Jesus teaches, is the ultimate expression of doing things right. To love, in this context, means to understand God's love, accept God's love, respect God's love, *and* express God's love. Love for God and for others leads to right thinking, whereas 'love' without God leads to wrong thinking and, inevitably, to disillusion and depression" (Brandt, 1988).

True happiness can only be experienced in the full intensity and warmth of God's selfless love. We must become channels of that love in the lives of our spouses, children, relatives, friends, neighbors, and so forth. Only God's love can so revolutionize our lives that we can learn to love others selflessly. Empowered by the Holy Spirit, we will be able to reach out to others, unhesitatingly and fully caring. And as we extend ourselves to some of the literally millions of individuals who are in need of God's love, we will find more meaning and purpose in our lives.

We must never say that there is nothing, or no one, to live for. Countless indeed are those who need a helping hand, a smile, a visit, or a phone call. Many are the lonely and grief-stricken who hunger for selfless love. If we extend ourselves beyond ourselves, and wholeheartedly focus on the great commandment of loving God and others as ourselves, we will find true happiness. A happiness that will last as long as we continue to rejoice in the God of our salvation: "Rejoice in the Lord always. I will say it again: Rejoice! Let your gentleness be evident to all. The Lord is near. Do not be anxious about anything, but in everything, by prayer and petition, with thanksgiving, present your requests to God. And the peace of God, which transcends all understanding, will guard your hearts and your minds in Christ Jesus" (Phil. 4:4–7).

Pray Without Ceasing

"Be joyful always; pray continually; give thanks in all circumstances, for this is God's will for you in Christ Jesus"(1 Thess. 5:16–18).

Absolutely nothing of spiritual value will materialize in our lives without prayer. It is not possible to have *salvation* (preservation from eternal misery), *sanctification* (freedom from the dominion of sin), or any other aspect of Christian transformation without earnestly requesting these blessings directly from God. As believers, we are commanded to be persistent in our prayers (1 Thess. 5:17) and reminded that the prayers of the righteous will be heard (Prov. 15:8,29). If we "humble ourselves, pray, seek God, and repent from our wickedness" (2 Chron. 7:14), then He will hear our requests and make us whole.

The effectiveness of our prayers rests not only on the selfless love of the One we petition, but also on that of the petitioner. God wants us to pray for things that are in accordance with His will and that will build up His Kingdom here on earth—a Kingdom of goodness, justice, righteousness, and of mercy and grace—a Kingdom of holiness and of conformity to the nature and will of God.

Numerous indeed are the scriptures that remind us that prayer is the key to happiness and all other aspects of emotional and spiritual wellness. Our prayers, however, must be in earnest and without ceasing. "Call to me," we read in Jeremiah (33:3), "and I will answer you and tell you great and unsearchable things you do not know." Our Heavenly Father rewards all who unwaveringly place their trust in Him: ". . . without faith it is impossible to please God, because anyone who comes to him must believe that he exists and that he rewards those who earnestly seek him" (Heb. 11:6). The more we trust and obey, the greater our happiness. In closing, let's briefly summarize this chapter.

The Secret of True Happiness

The secret of true happiness for a Christian is found in the selfless love of God and the power that flows from that love in every aspect of our daily life. The more we embrace God's love by fully trusting and obediently following Him, the more we can enjoy a deep-seated sense of contentment and joyfulness. True happiness rests squarely on something we can realistically validate and rationally evaluate. Our perceptions and cognitions have the final say whether we are going to be happy or not. Choice is involved in this process. Not everyone who hears about the selfless love of God is going to embrace that love, and not every Christian is going to fully trust and obey. But if we are willing to be led by the Holy Spirit, we will also enjoy the fruits of the Spirit, be endowed with power from on high, be surrounded with the sweet fragrance of God's presence, and discover the secret of true happiness: "The peace of God"—a peace beyond human understanding.

15

How to Have a Renewed Mind

Do not conform any longer to the pattern of this world, but be transformed by the renewing of your mind. Then you will be able to test and approve what God's will is—his good, pleasing and perfect will.

—Rom. 12:2

Next to salvation, there is hardly a more important or nobler goal than to seek a renewed mind. That goal, however, is neither quickly, nor easily reached. Once we have been wrestled from Satan's clutches, we joyfully start on our journey to excellence in Christ. But as soon as we take our first feeble steps on God's road to a transformed life, we discover that the road is all too often covered with potholes, filled with snares, lined with tempting billboards, marked with sinful detours, strewn with debris from the past, riddled with confusing turns, saddled with numerous stop signs, engulfed by distracting noise from fellow travelers, and blinded by lights from those who have elected to travel in the opposite direction and into the clutches of the great deceiver who continues to devour many a weary traveler.

The Renewed Mind

There are many reasons why it is so difficult to have a renewed (Christian) mind, and a transformed (Christian) life. Constantly faced with human fallibility, imperfections, and sinfulness, it is no surprise that many well-meaning individuals simply quit trying to have a renewed mind. Some of the more overlooked obstacles, however, are found in unhealthy personality traits and lifestyles. Those who believe that the renewed mind is a purely spiritual matter and must be seen completely separate from our brain are more likely to fail than those who clearly see a relationship between spirit, mind, brain, and body. For about twenty-five years, I have been involved directly in the lives of numerous Christians who could not get their spiritual lives in order until they started to pay sorely needed attention to the whole person.

Outwardly, many believers look as if their spiritual lives are just fine. They may regularly go to church, sing in the choir, hold functions in the church, be on boards or committees, be ministers, priests, or well-known Christian teachers; yet, they very often live lives of confusion, fear, and turmoil. This is a far bigger problem than is generally assumed. Those of us, however, who have been in the counseling profession for some time and have dealt with a wide range of problems, know that there are a lot of wounded and hurting individuals, regardless of their status in life, outward appearance, profession, or even their protestations. Early in my counseling career, I did not quite understand why so many faithful, God-fearing, wonderful servants of God could have so many unresolved problems, but gradually I learned that the difficulty often rested in their desire to be truly spiritual. They frequently failed to see that it is impossible to have a well-functioning spiritual mind without a well-functioning physical brain. They needed to pay attention to the whole person—spirit, mind, and body.

Earlier we looked at the necessity of taking good care of our bodies in order to have a healthy brain and an opportunity to develop a healthy mind. A healthy organic brain, we found, is essential for a healthy functional mind. While heredity and environment interact with each other in the development of our mind, we still have the final word. We are sometimes unhealthily conditioned

How to Have a Renewed Mind

and influenced as infants, children, and adolescents; but, eventually, most of us can choose to have a healthier mind—a mind that is more realistic than unrealistic, more rational than irrational, and more positive than negative. Regrettably, many individuals in our society are unaware of this choice, or they seem to ignore it. Perhaps some individuals simply fail to understand that a healthy mind is not inherited, but something we can achieve if we are willing to do a fair amount of work.

Most Christians might readily agree that it makes good sense to diligently search for a healthy lifestyle or a healthy personality style, but to work for a Christian mind and life may seem rather far-fetched, unspiritual, and even unscriptural. Since we have been "saved by grace through faith," and are "new creatures in Christ," it may indeed appear wrong, shameful, or sinful to work for a Christian mind. We have been touched by God the Father, God the Holy Spirit, and God the Son. What could we possibly do for ourselves? Salvation is, as we all know, a gift. The renewed mind is also a gift, at least in the sense that we cannot earn or purchase such a mind. But it is a gift for which we must prepare ourselves. Without conscious choices, commitment, or effort, it is not possible to have a Christian mind or a Christian lifestyle. God actually blesses us greatly by allowing us to be participators, doers, and fellow-heirs with Christ. Without our direct, conscious participation, there is neither accountability nor responsibility, neither growth nor victory.

Wise choices and sound decisions are truly essential if we are to have a healthy physical mental, emotional, social, or spiritual life. Many choices and decisions are sequential in nature. Our Christian spiritual life starts when we first listen to the call of God, respond to that call, renounce our sinful past, accept Christ, share our decision with others, seek to grow in our faith, learn about maturing in Christ, shed old habits and behaviors, renew our minds and have a transformed life. The Scriptures are quite clear that we are to be active participants in our Christian life. The renewed mind is built on a foundation of verbs!

Resisting the Darkness

"Do not conform," cries the apostle Paul, "any longer to the patterns of this world. . . . " Stop having that same outward appearance or inward disposition as those who are still living in darkness. Stop copying, imitating, and following the example of those who are lost. Stop living your life in the same manner as before you were redeemed by the blood of Christ, but rather, be transformed—changed into an entirely new person. And don't try to do that with some "whitewash." Don't put on a mask or try to fool yourself or others. Rather, change from within by the renewing of your mind. Have a fundamental change, and update your mind with a new way of thinking. Begin to think the way God thinks. Do that, and "you will be able to test and approve what God's will is . . ." God's will for your life, you will discover, is one that is ". . . good, pleasing and perfect . . ." (Rom. 12:2).

The apostle Paul is very clear that we can only have a transformed life if we have a renewed mind, and that we are to go after this mind with some passion. It is not a question of sitting back and waiting for God to bestow a new mind and new life on us, perhaps while we are lying on the couch and watching some "soap opera." Scripture after scripture throughout the New Testament, makes it abundantly clear that no one, but no one, will have a Christian mind or Christian lifestyle who does not actively want to have it and is not willing to work for it.

We must actively resist the evils that surround us and firmly reject the notion that whatever the majority does cannot be all wrong. *Majorities can be all wrong and often are.* Majorities have supported, if not always elected, some of the most murderous dictators of the twentieth century. And in our own country, so-called opinion polls indicate that a majority of the people will shamelessly support leaders with major character flaws as long as they provide them with plenty of economic prosperity. Character flaws apparently are only unacceptable if these leaders fail to deliver the "cake." It would seem that the character of these supporters may be more flawed than the character of the leaders they gladly support for personal gain. All of this is diametrically opposed to the Word of God (cf. Ps. 34:14, 97:10, 101:4; Prov. 8:13; Isa. 5:20).

The Scriptures remind us that while we are not to recompense evil for evil (Rom. 12:17; 1Thess. 5:15), we must hate it (Ps. 97:10), and overcome it (Rom. 12:21). In dealing with any kind of evil—especially in ourselves—let us carefully heed God's warnings: "Woe to those who call evil good and good evil . . ." (Isa. 5:20), and "Woe to those who . . . acquit the guilty for a bribe, but deny justice to the innocent" (Isa. 5:22,23). Unless we stand against evil, we cannot stand for good. We stand for nothing!

Dwelling in Darkness

In an earlier chapter, we looked at various unhealthy personality styles that stand in the way of a renewed mind and transformed life. These unhealthy personality styles can be powerful obstacles to *both* a constructive secular or Christian personality. The latter is, of course, impossible to attain unless all vestiges of Satan's power are removed from our life. An excellent way to prepare ourselves for a renewed mind is to know something about the various minds of darkness described in the Scriptures. Let's have a look at some of these minds.

THE BLINDED MIND

The blinded mind is a mind closed to spiritual truth. It is firmly in the grasp of a sinful world—a world of unbelievers who cannot see the light that is shining all around them. The blinded mind reminds us that we do not see with our eyes, nor hear with our ears, but see and hear, if we are ready to do so, with our minds. We must not allow Satan to blind our minds with self-defeating and self-destructive thoughts, feelings, and actions that will prevent us from seeing the truth.

Those who have a blinded mind can be face-to-face with miracles, yet be totally oblivious to them. All too many individuals allow Satan to sow the sand of deception in their eyes. Unless we submit ourselves to Christ, we fail to see the light of the gospel: "And even if our gospel is veiled, it is veiled to those who are

THE RENEWED MIND

perishing. The god of this age has blinded the minds of unbelievers, so that they cannot see the light of the gospel of the glory of Christ, who is the image of God" (2 Cor. 4:3–4).

THE CARNAL MIND

The carnal mind is a very common mind. It is the mind of the world—a mind whose roots are found in physical, rather than spiritual, things. It is often a grossly sensual, unchaste, and wanton mind—a mind that concerns itself mainly with material, temporal, and unholy matters. The carnal mind is dead set against doing the will of God. The apostle Paul points out that some "new" Christians may still have a carnal mind: ". . . since there is jealousy and quarreling among you, are you not worldly?" (1 Cor. 3:3).

In our society, scores of individuals are swept up by worldliness. We are surrounded by "experts" in government, education, and other institutions who are masters at "spinning" the truth, presenting corrupt practices as normal, peddling false doctrines as authentic, and "whitewashing" immoral behaviors as mere "errors in judgment." The Scriptures are clear on what we need to do. We are to separate ourselves in love from those who prefer a carnal mind over a spiritual mind, unrighteousness over righteousness, unholiness over holiness, and lies over truth. God desires that we keep ourselves free from worldly pollution (James 1:27) and reminds us that there is no fellowship between light and darkness (2 Cor. 6:14).

It is not possible to have any love for the carnal world or anything outside the will of God or His realm: "Do not love the world or anything in the world. If anyone loves the world, the love of the Father is not in him. For everything in the world—the cravings of sinful man, the lust of his eyes, and the boasting of what he has and does—comes not from the Father but from the world" (1 John. 2:15,16). The world includes anything, or anyone, associated with evil, or opposed to God. Those who are still conforming to the world, and making little, if any, effort to overcome it, or are unwilling to die to it (Gal. 6:14), are outside the will of God. Whatever our outward appearance, church attendance, or the so-called "good" works we do, if we have a carnal mind, we walk in darkness, and we are lost: "The mind of sinful man is death," cries the apostle Paul, "but the mind controlled by the Spirit is life and peace. . . ." (Rom. 8:6).

THE DEFILED MIND

The defiled mind is a mind filled with evil thoughts, words, and deeds. The Scriptures teach that the defiled mind is an unclean mind that has *voluntarily* been placed under the control of Satan. We are reminded here once again of our accountability and responsibility. We are responsible for the choices we make. In spite of genetic or environmental influences, the vast majority of individuals are capable of choosing either good or evil. "In his heart," we read in Proverbs 16:9, "a man plans his course. . . ." As for evil, we are reminded that this comes from within ourselves (Matt. 15:19).

It is incorrect to blame other people, Satan, or our environment, for the many evil things that *we* do. In our modern society, it is common place for individuals to falsely blame others for the evil things they are doing. As explained throughout this book, we are responsible for our behavior (cf. Jer. 17:4–10; Matt. 15:19–20). This is what Jesus said about the defiled mind: "What comes out of a man is what makes him 'unclean.' For from within, out of men's hearts, come evil thoughts, sexual immorality, theft, murder, adultery, greed, malice, deceit, lewdness, envy, slander, arrogance and folly. All these evils come from inside and make a man 'unclean'" (Mark. 7:20–23).

THE DEPRAVED MIND

The depraved mind is so self-destructive that it does not seem to care about the terrible immorality that springs from it. Without obedience to God's holy standards, there can only be moral depravity. While God never leaves us, nor forsakes us (Josh. 1:5; Heb. 13:5), He does not force us to go His way. If we forsake Him, then we have isolated ourselves by our own choice (2 Chron. 15:2). God gives us the freedom to choose good or evil, life or death. The Scriptures are very clear, and human history fully confirms, that immorality is the one sure road to death and destruction (cf. Rom. 1:18–32).

Depravity comes directly from Satan—who seeks to corrupt what is good, spoil what is perfect, and render worthless what is of value. In his letter to the Romans, the apostle Paul leaves no room for misinterpretation that sexual immorality, strife deceit, malice, slander, gossip, or disobedience to parents, all come from one and the same source. Please note that those who have a depraved mind fail to be contrite, fail to change their ways, and will justify their immorality: "Although they know God's righteous decree that those who do such things deserve death, they not only continue to do these very things but also approve of those who practice them" (Rom. 1:32).

The Doubtful Mind

The doubtful mind is a perpetually divided mind. It is uncertain because it tries to function in two or more contradictory worlds. There are many individuals who constantly waver between one thing or another. The doubtful mind's lack of confidence is often seen in suspicion and confusion. It lacks direction and may do one thing on a given day, only to do the exact opposite on the next day, without knowing for sure if it is right to do so or not. The doubtful mind will also attempt to do contrary things at the same time—for example, serve God and Money (Matt. 6:24).

The Scriptures are quite clear that God wants us to live by faith—faith based on truth and reason, anchored solidly in the Word of God, richly verified by history, and joyfully experienced by all who know that "Every good and perfect gift is from above, coming down from the Father of the heavenly lights, who does not change like shifting shadows" (James 1:17). When all is said and done, and the limitations of our reasoning minds become evident, we must find ourselves on the immovable rock of revealed truth—a rock that has come down to us as yet another gift from God—a gift of faith, allowing us to be aglow with an unshakable and joyful confidence, expectation, fidelity, and optimism.

God reminds us that a wavering mind is self-defeating and unproductive. He cannot help us when we come to Him with such a mind: "If any of you lacks wisdom, he should ask God, who gives generously to all without finding fault, and it will be given to him. But when he asks, he must believe and not doubt, because he who doubts is like a wave of the sea, blown and tossed by the wind. That man should not think he will receive anything from the Lord; he is a double-minded man, unstable in all he does" (James 1:5–8).

Dwelling in Light
The only cure for darkness is light, and the only cure for a self-defeating mind is a renewed mind. A renewed mind is "the mind of Christ within us." An escape from deadly darkness for lost souls can only be found in our Lord and Savior Jesus Christ. He alone is ". . . the way and the truth and the life" (John. 14:6), and He alone is the gate through which we can enter into the glorious light of the gospel: "I am the gate; whoever enters through me will be saved" (John 10:9).

Salvation by grace through faith assures us of eternal life, but, as we have already learned, it does not necessarily assure us of a personality makeover. God is looking for doers. He wants us to follow in His footsteps. He is looking for participators, not spectators. If we desire a transformed life, we must work for it. God holds us responsible to remove sinful strongholds from our lives, including the removal of a blinded, carnal, depraved, defiled, doubtful, or any other self-defeating or destructive mind.

How wonderful it is to dwell in the life-giving and life-protecting light of God: "The Lord is my light and my salvation—whom shall I fear?" (Ps. 27:1). Indeed, of whom are we to be afraid if we walk in that all-powerful "light of the Lord" (Isa. 2:5). His light exceeds the light of the stars, the brightness of the moon, and the splendor of the sun. Nothing can match the light of the Lord; it penetrates deep into the hearts and minds of all who are willing to receive it. It is only when our minds are illuminated with the love and light of Christ, that we can begin to grasp a little about the extent of God's selfless love.

Dwelling in Love
The renewed mind is an updated Christian mind; a mind that has repented of greed, selfishness, and every evil thing; a mind that, in loving communion with God, daily prepares itself to selflessly serve Him and others. All who are believers in, and followers of Jesus Christ, the Son of God, can receive a renewed mind. This wonderful event, however, calls for a faithful commitment to embrace God's love actively and passively. It requires that we allow God's love to shine in our own lives, and the lives of others, through righteous living and other Christian attributes (Eph 4:25–32; 5:8,9; Col. 3:12–17; Gal. 5:22–26).

In this book, I have stressed the importance of constructive thinking (truth, reason, and faith); a healthy personality style (insight, openness, and flexibility); and, wholesome living (diet, exercise, and relaxation). Since there are no "zippers" between our spiritual, emotional, and physical life, we have to deal with the total person (1 Thess. 5:23). Some may fail to see a connection between a healthy physical, emotional, and spiritual life, but this does not alter the facts. Having said all of this, we need to remember that, in final analysis, we must learn to think primarily in terms of love, the great all-inclusive commandment.

In order to have a mind of light and love, we must do away with our old self-defeating minds. It is something that each person must do for him or herself, and which may require some intense soul-searching. We must make sure that all vestiges of doubtful, defiled, carnal, or other unacceptable minds are eradicated from our life. "Put to death, therefore," God tells us, "whatever belongs to your earthly nature: sexual immorality, impurity, lust, evil desires and greed, which is idolatry. Because of these, the wrath of God is coming. You used to walk in these ways, in the life you once lived. But now you must rid yourselves of all such things as these: anger, rage, malice, slander, and filthy language from your lips" (Col. 3:5–8).

There are lots of other evil (corrupt, immoral, malicious) things that we must rid ourselves of. But rather than focusing on lengthy lists of evil, we had best focus on how God wants us to think and live: ". . . as God's chosen people, holy and dearly loved, clothe yourselves with compassion, kindness, humility, gentleness, and patience. Bear with each other and forgive whatever grievances you may have against one another. Forgive as the Lord forgave you. And over all these virtues put on love, which binds them all together in perfect unity" (Col. 3:12–14). The emphasis in these scriptures is clear: We must love one another.

Love is an indispensable emotion. Love is a choice, decision, thought, attitude, way of life, and so much more. God's very essence is love: "God is love. Whoever lives in love lives in God, and God in him" (1 John. 4:16). Oswald Chambers (1989) wrote "(love) never came from the devil and never can go to the devil. When I am rightly related to God, the more I love, the more blessing does He pour out on other lives. The reward of love is the capacity to pour out more love all the time . . ." And that, indeed, is the wondrous nature of love. The more we give it away, the more of it we have."

How true it is that the more we focus on the selfless love of God, and the more we practice it, the more we experience its power. Love is a mighty power that comforts, heals, and rescues. It is a powerful light in a dark and selfish world—a power expressed in such traits as forgiveness, generosity, kindness, mercy, patience, peacefulness, and truthfulness. It is a power that can radically change us and revolutionize our relationships with others. To love is the ultimate expression of doing things right. It means we understand God's love, accept God's love, respect God's love, and express God's love.

As human beings, we can never do justice to the love of God. We can perhaps best sing of its surpassing wonder. But here I am reduced to writing in prose that which staggers us. It also staggered Hosea, whose prophesy resounds with the intensity of a love that is shown even to those who are wickedly unresponsive to it (Hos. 11; Is. 19:24). God's love, as so beautifully set forth in

Matthew, Mark, and Luke, is the key note of the kingdom Jesus ushered in. It is in John's gospel (John. 3:16) that we encounter the golden text of the Bible: "For God so loved the world that he gave his one and only Son . . ." a love extended to the whole world but experienced in is full intensity only by believers, who are not only the recipients of love, but also the channels by which it affects their relatives, friends, and neighbors.

The Renewed Mind

"Next to salvation," I said earlier in this chapter, "there is hardly a nobler goal than to seek a renewed mind." There is also not a more urgent goal. Unhealthy personalities and "minds of darkness" are behind virtually all of our personal and interpersonal unhappiness and behind most of the anger, bitterness, hatred, violence, and every other form of wickedness that tears our world and civilization apart. All of this could be dramatically changed if more individuals would be obedient to "the God of Abraham, Isaac, and Jacob." Here Christian, Jew, and Muslim alike have a common meeting ground: A Holy God who *abounds in love* (Exod. 34:6) and who *exhorts us to love one another* (Lev. 19:18,34). Let us be as unfailing in our love to one another—whatever our cultural, religious, or denominational background—as God is toward everyone of us (Ps. 33:5).

The renewed mind, as described by the apostle Paul in the book of Romans and elsewhere, is certainly a major challenge that God places before all who have accepted Jesus Christ as Lord and Savior. As Christians, we are reminded that being "saved by grace," and "justified by faith," does not exclude our active and obedient participation in our spiritual growth. A spiritual growth that is unattainable except through the selfless love of God the Father, the redeeming love of God the Son, and the guiding love of God the Holy Spirit.

The challenge of a renewed mind comes with a wonderful promise: A transformed life filled with vibrant faith, the joyful indwelling of the Holy Spirit, and the continual presence of the love of Christ. A renewed mind and transformed life deals with the whole person. It deals with wellness for body, mind and spirit; with salvation, justification, and sanctification; with truth, reason and faith; and, with self-consecration—a consecration that results in a life of godliness. This is a life that is pleasing to God, helpful to ourselves and others, and which reflects a happy obedience to God's earnest and loving plea to be wholehearted doers of what He teaches us: "But the man who looks intently into the perfect law that gives freedom, and continues to do this, not forgetting what he has heard, but doing it—he will be blessed in what he does" (James 1:25).

The call for all believers to seek a renewed mind is as urgent today as when the apostle Paul wrote his letter to the church at Rome nearly two thousand years ago. There was, and there is, confusion among many followers of Christ—among those who believe that righteousness demands a set of legalistic rules and those who say it only consists of a passive state of blessedness. Our righteousness is not self-righteousness, but a right relationship with God (Rom. 3:20–31)—a relationship based on faith in Jesus Christ as Lord and Savior: "For in the gospel a righteousness from God is revealed, a righteousness that is by faith from first to last, just as it is written: 'The righteous will live by faith'" (Rom. 1:17). There is no question that we are ". . . justified by faith apart from observing the law" (Rom. 3:28).

There is also no question, however, that we are called to obedience. After explaining that our righteousness is through faith, the Apostle cries out: "Do we then nullify the law by this faith? Not at all! Rather, we uphold the law" (Rom. 3:31). There is no inconsistency between being saved and justified by faith and God's urging to *walk* in the newness of life—a newness that can only be experienced by our willingness to be cleansed and consecrated; to be renewed and transformed. We find a pressing plea to cleanse ourselves from worldly strongholds and experience the fullness of God's will for our lives.

> Therefore, I urge you, brothers, in view of God's mercy, to offer your bodies as *living sacrifices*, holy and pleasing to God—this is your *spiritual* act of worship. Do not conform any longer to

the pattern of this world, but be transformed by the renewing of your mind. *Then* you will be able to test and approve what God's will is—his good, pleasing and perfect will. (Rom.12:1–2; italics added)

There are many good reasons to offer all of ourselves to God. In the foregoing scriptures, however, we find only three reasons advanced for a godly life. First, God has shown his *loving mercy* toward us—a mercy that is great indeed, for we have been created in His image, purchased by His blood, endowed with His power, and continually blessed with His loving kindness and faithfulness. Second, it is *pleasing* to God. Who of the "redeemed of the Lord" is not desirous to do whatever is pleasing to God? Surely our goal is to please God (2 Cor. 5:9) and consecrating ourselves to God is both an implied command (Lev. 19:2) and a tremendous blessing to others as well as to ourselves. Last, it is our *spiritual* (reasonable) *service* to live a life of godliness. It is definitely a rational act for any redeemed person to present his or her body to God; to serve and worship Him with both spirit and mind—a worship that is acceptable to God because it is done with both our spirit and our understanding.

When our minds have been touched by the love of Christ, we most gladly present our bodies as useful instruments—bodies in which we are diminished and Christ is magnified. As Christians, we must be eager to do what is good. Our lives are to be marked by benevolence, courtesy, forgiveness, friendliness, generosity, goodness, helpfulness, humbleness, kindness, mercy, patience, peacefulness, and unselfishness toward others. A Christian's spiritual fitness, however, while firmly founded on faith in Christ and salvation by grace, is solely manifested by godly fruits. We are to live gracefully, and gratefully, by the love, voice, will, spirit, and mind of God.

We can only have the mind of Christ after we remove our old sinful character traits and replace them with new Christian traits, such as: devotion, faithfulness, honesty, integrity, moderation, prayer, and purity. It is not possible to have a transformed life without first having a renewed mind. The latter is an ongoing, lifelong process—one that involves the removal of every selfish evil and stronghold within us.

Unless we abhor evil and embrace good, we shall find ourselves in the middle of the "suspension bridge of life," swaying back and forth over a treacherous ravine filled with sinful distractions and urges, tempting us to let go of our lifeline in Christ and forfeit God's blessings. We must be steadfast so that we can cry out with Timothy: "I have fought the good fight, I have finished the race, I have kept the faith. Now there is in store for me the crown of righteousness, which the Lord, the righteous Judge, will award to me on that day—and not only to me, but also to all who have longed for his appearing" (2 Tim. 4:7–8).

References

Abrahamson, E. M., and A. W. Pezet. (1977). *Body, Mind, and Sugar.* New York: Avon Books.

Anderson, Robert A. (1990). *Wellness Medicine.* New Canaan, CT: Keats Publishing Inc.

Balch, James F., and Phyllis A. Balch. (1997). *Prescription for Nutritional Healing.* Garden City Park, NY: Avery Publishing Group.

Baker, Elizabeth. (1997). *Does The Bible Teach Nutrition?* Mukilteo, WA: WinePress Publishing.

Bauer, J. (1982). *Clinical Laboratory Methods.* St. Louis: C. V. Mosby Company.

Brandt, Frans M. J. (1977). *A Rational Self-Counseling Primer.* Kelsale Court, Saxmundham, Suffolk, England: Institute for Rational Therapy.

Brandt, Frans M. J. (1978). *A Guide to Rational Weight Control.* Kelsale Court, Saxmundham, Suffolk, England: Institute for Rational Therapy.

Brandt, Frans M. J. (1984). *The Way to Wholeness.* Westchester, IL: Crossway Books.

Brandt, Frans M. J. (1988). *Victory Over Depression.* Grand Rapids, MI: Baker Book House.

Brandt, Frans M. J. (1992). *The Psychology of Personal Excellence.* Paper presented at the Bilateral Conference of the American Counseling Association and the Moray House Institute of Education, Heriot-Watt University, Edinburgh.

Brandt, Frans M. J. (1992). *The Diagnosis and Treatment of Personality Disorders.* Paper presented to the National Council of Psychotherapists, Royal Society of Medicine, London.

Brandt, Frans M. J. (1998). *Personality and Love*. East Tawas, MI: Brandt Human Development Consulting.
Carlson, Carole C. (1983). *Corrie ten Boom: Her Live, Her Faith*. Old Tappan, NJ: Fleming H. Revell Company.
Cleave, T. L. (1974). *The Saccharine Disease*. New Canaan, CT: Keats Publishing, Inc.
Diagnostic and Statistical Manual of Mental Disorders, DSM-IV (1994). Washington: American Psychiatric Association.
Eareckson, Joni. (1976). *Joni*. Minneapolis: World Wide Publications.
Forbes, Alex. (1984). *The Bristol Diet*. London: Century Publishing House.
Fingarette, Herbert. (1988). *Heavy Drinking*, Berkeley, CA: University of California Press.
Gordon, S. D. (1903). *Quiet Talks on Power*. New York: Grosset & Dunlap.
Graham, Billy. (1978). *The Holy Spirit*. Waco TX: Word Books.
Gustafson, Axel. (1884). *The Foundation of Death*. London: Kegan, Paul, Trench & Co.
Jones, Peter. (1997). *Spirit Wars*. Mukilteo, WA: WinePress Publishing.
Kaplan, Harold I., and Benjamin J. Sadock. (1985). *Comprehensive Textbook of Psychiatry/IV.* Baltimore, MD: William Wilkins.
Keller, Helen. (1954). *The Story of My Life*. Garden City, NY: Doubleday Company, Inc.
Lewis, C. S. (1949). *The Weight of Glory and Other Addresses*. New York: MacMillan Co.
Light, Marilyn H. ed. (1980). *Hypoadrenocorticism*. Troy, NY: Adrenal Metabolic Research Society of the Hypoglycemia Foundation, Inc.
Millon, Theodore. (1996). *Disorders of Personality, DSM-IV and Beyond*. New York: John Wisely & Sons, Inc.
Murray, Michael, T., and Joseph E. Pizzorno. (1991). *Encyclopedia of Natural Medicine*. Rockline, CA: Prima Publishing.
PDR for Herbal Medicines (1999). Montvale, NJ: Medical Economics Company, Inc.
Rodale, J.I. (1968). *Natural Health, Sugar and the Criminal Mind*. New York: Pyramid Books.
Roland, Per E. (1993). *Brain Activation*. New York: Wiley-Liss, Inc.
Schauss, Alexander (1981). *Diet, Crime and Delinquency*. Berkeley, CA: Parker House.
Smith, Hannah Whitall. (1952). *The Christian's Secret of a Happy Life*. Westwood, NJ: Fleming H. Revell Company.
The Amplified Bible. (1987). Grand Rapids: Zondervan Bible Publishers.
Yudkin, John. (1972). *Sweet and Dangerous*. New York: Wyden Publishers.

Subject Index

Ability to reason. *See* choice
Actual Practice, 80–84
Alcohol, dangers of, 89–90, 93, 106–108
Anger, 58–59, 78, 94
Antisocial personality, 59–61, 78, 94, 133–134, 148
Anxiety, 59–61, 78, 94
Avoidant personality, 134–135
Believers, Christian, 46, 49, 90, 130, 179, 185, 186
Blinded mind, 185, 186
Borderline personality, 135–137, 148
Caffeine, dangers of, 108–111
Capricious and unstable persons. *See* Borderline personality
Caring persons, 154–155
Carnal mind, 46–47, 186–187
Christian Cognitive Therapy, 65
Civilization, Christian, 20–21
Choice, 29–32, 52–53, 67–68, 78–84, 164–165, 171–180, 189–195
Critical and perfectionistic persons. *See* Compulsive personality
Comfortable persons, 158–160
Compulsive personality, 137–139
Constructive persons, 155–158
Constructive thinking, 22, 41, 153–158, 190
Counseling, Christian, 27–29
Deceitful and uncaring persons. *See* Antisocial Personality
Defiled mind, 187
Dependent personality, 139–140
Depraved mind, 187–188
Depression, 61–63, 73, 95
Depressive personality, 148–149
Depressive illness, 61
Detached and unsociable persons. *See* Schizoid personality
Diet, importance of, 87–89, 92–93, 119–123
Doubtful mind, 188–189
Dramatic and impulsive persons. *See* Histrionic personality

Egotistical and exploitative persons. *See* Narcissistic personality
Emotions, understanding, 57–65
Emotional insight, 83
Emotional problems, physical roots of, 94–102
Emotional re-education, 78–84
Exercise, importance of, 117–118
Faith, 35–42, 192–195
Glucose, importance of, 95–102
God-confusion, 24; God-neglect, 24; God-void, 24, 60, 70
Happiness, 163–180; false, 167–180; Rx for, 171–180; true, 168–171; secret of, 180
Healthy personality, 151–161
Histrionic personality, 140–141, 148
Holy Spirit, 43–50
Hypersensitive and withdrawn persons. *See* Avoidant personality
Hypervigilant and suspicious persons. *See* Paranoid personality
Hypoglycemia, 95–102
Illness, lifestyle and, 87–102; chronic, sources of, 89–90
Insecure and clinging persons. *See* Dependent personality
Intellectual insight, 78, 79
Jesus, 24, 30, 35, 39–41, 45–49, 69, 72, 75, 76, 169, 174–175, 177–179, 183–184, 189–195
Joy, 63–64
Lifestyle, healthy, 115–126
Love, 177–178
Low blood sugar, symptoms of, 98–99
Mental practice. *See* Vicarious practice
Narcissistic personality, 141–142
Negativistic personality, 143–144

Nicotine, dangers of. *See* Tobacco, dangers of
Obsessive-Compulsive Disorder, 139
Oppositional and vacillating persons. *See* Negativistic personality
Optimism, 157–158
Paranoid personality, 144–147
Personality, Christian. *See* Renewed mind
Personality, healthy, 152, 153; unhealthy, 129–131
Pessimistic and cheerless persons. *See* Depressive personality
Positive thinking, faith and, 35–36
Prayer, 179
Rational. *See* Reason
Realistic thinking, 155–156
Reason, 35–42, 156–157
Renewed mind, 181–195
Sanctification, 53, 181–185, 193–195
Salvation, 21, 24, 41, 53, 70–73, 183, 189, 192
Self-abasing persons. *See* Self-defeating personality
Self-counseling, Christian, 27–29
Self-defeating personality, 149–150
Self-talk, 77–78
Schizoid personality, 147–148
Sleeplessness, 118–119
Spirit-filled life, the, 46–49
Spiritual anxiety, antidote to, 60–61
Sugar, dangers of, 111–113
Tobacco, dangers of, 89–90, 105–106
Vicarious practice, 80–82
Wellness diet, 119–123